WE LIVE

Other Works by Father Oscar Lukefahr

"We Believe..." A Survey of the Catholic Faith

We Worship: A Guide to the Cathoic Mass

We Pray: Living in God's Presence

A Catholic Guide to the Bible

The Privilege of Being Catholic

The Catechism Handbook

Christ's Mother and Ours

The Search for Happiness

WE LIVE

TO KNOW, LOVE, AND SERVE GOD

Father Oscar Lukefahr, CM

Foreword by
Bishop James V. Johnston, Jr.

Liguori
LIGUORI, MISSOURI

Imprimi Potest:
Thomas D. Picton, C.Ss.R.
Provincial, Denver Province
The Redemptorists

Published by Liguori Publications
Liguori, Missouri
To order, call 800-325-9521
www.liguori.org

Scripture citations are from the New Revised Standard Version of the Bible, copyright 1989 by the Division of Christian Education of the National Council of Churches of Christ in the USA. All rights reserved. Used with permission.

Excerpts from the English translation of the *Catechism of the Catholic Church* for the United States of America copyright © 1994, United States Catholic Conference, Inc.—Libreria Editrice Vaticana. English translation of the *Catechism of the Catholic Church: Modifications from the Editio Typica* copyright © 1997, United States Catholic Conference, Inc.—Libreria Editrice Vaticana.

Liguori Publications, a nonprofit corporation, is an apostolate of the Redemptorists. To learn more about the Redemptorists, visit Redemptorists.com.

Printed in the United States of America
14 13 12 11 10   5 4 3 2 1
First edition

DEDICATION

To Rob and Sallie Hurley
Thank you!

ACKNOWLEDGMENTS

Sincere thanks to all who helped in the writing of this book: to Liguori editorial director, Jay Staten, who oversaw this project; to Christine Navarro, for editing; to Pam Hummelsheim, for cover and page design; to Dianna Graveman, for copy editing; to Rob and Sallie Hurley for advice and encouragement; to Paul and Carol Berens, Mike and Mary Etta Dunaway, Frank and Gail Jones, and Den and Kathy Vollink, who discussed each chapter at our monthly study group meetings; to Carol Berens for proofreading and advice; to Penny Elder, Cheryl Callier, and Sherrie Hotop for proofreading and suggestions. And I am especially grateful to the Most Reverend James V. Johnston, Bishop of Springfield-Cape Girardeau, for writing the foreword. May God bless you all!

FOREWORD

In Saint Paul's well-known speech to the Athenians in the Areopagus, he noted: "From one ancestor he made all nations to inhabit the whole earth, and he allotted the times of their existence and the boundaries of the places where they would live, so that they would search for God and perhaps grope for him and find him—though indeed he is not far from each one of us. For 'In him we live and move and have our being'..." (Acts 17:26–28). In these words, the Apostle to the Gentiles sums up the mighty quest that is at the heart of every person's identity and existence. This quest begins not with us but with God, who first loved us and pursues us as the "hound of heaven," to use the poetic imagery from Francis Thompson's famous poem. God's goodness and grace moves our hearts to seek him in response.

In his extensive work as a pastor, preacher, retreat master, and teacher, Father Oscar Lukefahr, CM, has developed a remarkable gift for helping others in this great quest. This book, *We Live: To Know, Love, And Serve God*, is another contribution to his quest. It has several attributes that make it eminently readable and helpful, and all are common to Father Lukefahr's work.

First, the content is solid. *We Live* is rooted in what might be called "meat and potatoes" Catholic teaching. In reading this book, the reader is immersed in both the Bible and the solid doctrine of the Church as expressed in the *Catechism of the Catholic Church*.

Second, there is the down to earth simplicity and clarity that every skilled teacher is able to bring to a subject. *We Live* brings truth to life through Father Lukefahr's entertaining style, which draws from his and others' experiences in everyday life. Father also adds his own love and fascination with scientific discovery and research. The book possesses that remarkable quality of common sense examples to provide "windows" into the wondrous mystery of God and his love and action in our lives.

We Live accomplishes what many a good book has done: it draws the reader into the adventure. In the end, every person who has met the Lord and encountered his love is moved to set out on the adventure of discipleship. This is a capsule of the Christian life, and it is a pattern that is repeated in the life of every disciple. God invites, pursues, woos us as his beloved; and we respond—caught up in a love that is greater than ourselves, but which does not destroy us or take away our freedom. Rather, this love "impels us" (2 Corinthians 5:14) to be who we were created by God to be... our best selves.

In the first encyclical of his papacy, Pope Benedict XVI chose to expound on the great mystery of Divine Love, titling the document *Deus Caritas Est* (God is Love). In doing so, the Holy Father was drawing us back to this central truth about God, which in turn sheds the light of Revelation on the truth about ourselves, our purpose, our eternal destiny, and how to get there. One readily sees this theme reflected in *We Live.*

I believe this book will find many uses such as personal faith enrichment, use in parish Rite of Christian Initiation of Adults (RCIA) programs, and in adult education and faith sharing groups. Whether you are a new seeker or are already a disciple of the Lord Jesus Christ, I believe you will find this book to be a helpful addition to your ongoing adventure to seek, to find, and to follow the Lord along the narrow way that leads to true and everlasting life.

JAMES V. JOHNSTON, JR.
BISHOP OF SPRINGFIELD-CAPE GIRARDEAU

CONTENTS

INTRODUCTION

Some time ago, a member of the Liguori editorial staff pointed out that I had written books relating to three of the four pillars or main divisions of the *Catechism of the Catholic Church.* Part One, The Profession of Faith, is covered in *"We Believe...": A Survey of the Catholic Faith.* Part Two, The Celebration of the Christian Mystery, is discussed in *We Worship: A Guide to the Catholic Mass.* Part Four, Christian Prayer, is studied in *We Pray: Living in God's Presence.* "What about Part Three, Life in Christ?" asked the editor.

This book, *We Live: To Know, Love, and Serve God* is the answer to that question. Its title and structure are based on another question from the *Baltimore Catechism*: "Why did God make you?" and on its answer, "God made me to know him, to love him, and to serve him in this world, and to be happy with him forever in heaven."

God knows what is best for us. Discovering why we are here and following God's plan for our life makes good sense. It also brings peace and happiness, even in difficult circumstances. At a parish mission, I met an elderly and devout Catholic gentleman who had endured years of bad health and several open heart surgeries with seven bypasses. Yet his smile lit up the room. When I asked him why he was so happy, he answered, "How could I be anything but happy? Life is delicious!"

Some years ago I visited a good friend who was dying of brain cancer. Ken was slipping in and out of consciousness, and seemed also to be moving back and forth from this world to the next. His daughter told me that he was apparently returning from a visit to heaven as he whispered to her, "It's so beautiful."

Life can be an exciting venture filled with great possibilities when we realize that God made us to know, love, and serve him on earth and be happy with him in heaven. We can certainly describe it as beautiful, perhaps even as delicious.

The Catholic Church began on earth at the Annunciation with Jesus, though the Church had been in the Father's plan for all eternity. A retired teaching nun told me that on the Feast of the Annunciation she asked the children in her second grade class how the story of Christmas began. A little boy raised his hand and replied, "Well, it could begin in two ways, 'Once upon a time,' or 'Long, long ago.'"

Our purpose in life is not limited to history but originates in the loving heart of God, long, long ago! God has loved us from all eternity and calls us to find joy in his presence forever. In this book we'll consider God's eternal desire for union with us and his plan that the relationship will continue forever.

Let us "press on toward the goal for the prize of the heavenly call of God in Christ Jesus" (Philippians 3:14).

FATHER OSCAR LUKEFAHR, CM

CHAPTER I

God's Plan for Our Life in Christ

Why are you here? What is life's purpose? What is the meaning of life? If you do an Internet search on "the meaning of life," you'll get more than eighty million responses in half a second. Among those responses you'll find claims that life's meaning can be found in success, prosperity, fame, or achievement. You'll be advised to try this philosophy or that book. You'll be told (at various "atheist.com" sites) that life has no real meaning at all. You'll find humor, like the cartoon of a businessman addressing a guru on a mountain peak: "What is the meaning of life? But make it quick. I've got an important meeting in thirty minutes."

What *is* the meaning of life? Why are we here? What is life's purpose? When I was a child, the purpose of life was one of the first things taught in Catholic grade school. The *Baltimore Catechism* asked, "Why did God make you?" Generations of Catholic children learned the answer: "God made me to know him, to love him, and to serve him in this world, and to be happy with him forever in heaven."

This is an answer you can count on! It is God's answer, given in various ways throughout the Bible, taught by Jesus Christ, and treasured by the Catholic Church for twenty centuries. Why are you here? Because God made you.

So God created humankind in his image,
in the image of God he created them;
male and female he created them.

GENESIS 1:27

For what purpose did God make you?

TO KNOW, LOVE, AND SERVE GOD

God made you to **know** him. The Bible says, "And this is eternal life, that they may know you, the only true God, and Jesus Christ whom you have sent" (John 17:3).

God made you to **love** him. Jesus said, "You shall love the Lord your God with all your heart, and with all your soul, and with all your mind" (Matthew 22:37).

God made you to **serve** him. Jesus said, "Whoever serves me must follow me, and where I am, there will my servant be also. Whoever serves me, the Father will honor" (John 12:26).

God made you to be **happy** forever in heaven. Jesus said, "So you have pain now; but I will see you again, and your hearts will rejoice, and no one will take your joy from you" (John 16:22).

If you realize that life's purpose is knowing, loving, and serving God and finding happiness in God's presence, and if you make it your goal to know, love, and serve God, your life will have meaning. You may be single or married, prosperous or poor, young or old, healthy or not. Whatever your circumstances, you will find meaning and happiness if you know, love, and serve God.

BEING HAPPY FOREVER

You might say, "I want to be happy, of course. But this business of knowing, loving, and serving God doesn't sound very exciting. How is it supposed to make me happy forever?"

If this thought comes to mind, you might want to consider what knowing, loving, and serving other people can mean here and now. Look at how you enjoy being with friends and spending time with them. Think of an engaged couple growing in their knowledge and love of each other day-by-day. Picture parents holding a newborn child for the first time, welcoming that child to life and family, and loving that child so fiercely that they would die in defense of their little one. Recall times when you found satisfaction and joy in working for a good cause, helping friends, serving members of your family.

Consider all these occasions of knowing, loving, and serving, as well as the happiness they bring. Multiply these instances by billions, and you'll begin to have some notion of how knowing, loving, and serving God can make you happy now and forever.

Or think of people like Mother Teresa. She radiated joy from the experience of knowing, loving, and serving God. Such joy is not meant only for saints. It is meant for us all. We, unfortunately, don't always grasp why we're here as clearly as do the saints, but we can learn from them.

Another insight into the purpose of life is provided by people who have had near-death experiences. Because of accident or illness, their heartbeat and other vital functions ceased. They died. In the accounts of many such experiences, individuals describe leaving their body and watching doctors working frantically to bring them back to this life. Upon being revived, they tell of experiencing the presence of God and being enveloped in an ineffable sense of peace and joy. Many report that they learned from clinical death what really matters in this life and beyond: knowledge and love.

It's really true. God made you to know, love, and serve him in this world, and to be happy with him forever in heaven. So don't waste time considering the other eighty million ideas from the Internet about the meaning of life. God invented human life. God gives life meaning and knows its purpose.

OLD CATECHISM AND NEW

The newer *Catechism of the Catholic Church* further develops what the *Baltimore Catechism* taught about God's plan for us.

God, infinitely perfect and blessed in himself, in a plan of sheer goodness, freely created man to make him share in his own blessed life. To accomplish this, when the fullness of time had come, God sent his Son as Redeemer and Savior. In his Son and through him, he invites men to become, in the Holy Spirit, his adopted children and thus heirs of his blessed life (CCC 1). All Christ's faithful are called to hand it on from generation to generation, by professing the faith, by living it in fraternal sharing, and by celebrating it in liturgy and prayer (CCC 3).

If you want your life to be exciting, purposeful, and happy, follow God's "plan of sheer goodness." In this book, we will explore what it means to know, love, and serve God. We'll discuss the many ways of getting to know God: through nature, the Bible, other people, and above all through the mind and heart of Jesus Christ. Jesus is the one who can teach us how to know and love God, especially through prayer and worship. Jesus shows by word and example that to serve other people is to serve God. Such service, by the grace of God, will bring us to eternal joy (Matthew 25). It's a great plan. It's God's plan for our life and for our happiness.

TRUSTING GOD

Can we trust God's plan? I have been a priest for over forty years, and I've never been disappointed by God's plan of sheer goodness revealed in Jesus. I've talked with thousands of people about the meaning of life, and I've never heard anyone express regret for following Jesus.

You are invited to come along on this journey of faith to study God's answers to the questions life poses. It's a fascinating journey, mapped out in the Bible and the Church, with Jesus as our Way, Truth, and Life. At the end, we'll find, as Saint Augustine did centuries ago: "You have made us for yourself, O Lord, and our hearts are restless until they rest in you."

QUESTIONS FOR DISCUSSION AND REFLECTION

When was the last time you considered questions like, "Why am I here?" "What is the meaning of life?" Have you ever experienced a significant setback, such as the death of a loved one, that made you ask such questions? Do you have any friends or relatives who "radiate joy" from knowing, loving, and serving God?

ACTIVITIES

In a time of silent prayer, consider the four Scripture passages found in the section, "To Know, Love, and Serve God." Place yourself in the presence of Jesus and ask him to speak these words to your heart. Then respond to Jesus, asking him to help you know, love, and serve him in this life and to be happy with him forever in heaven.

CHAPTER 2

Is There a God to Be Known?

"God made us to know him." If we are to consider the issue of knowing God seriously, we must first consider whether there is a God to be known. Today, polls show that the vast majority of people believe in God. But there are also atheists, those who deny God's existence.

Nobody talks more about God than atheists do, and they can be shrill and desperate. In his book, *The God Delusion*, Richard Dawkins rails against believers, scorning them for believing what he says is only a "delusion." Dawkins claims that parents who teach religion to their children are guilty of child abuse. He declares that no intelligent person feels the need for the supernatural, unless he or she was brought up that way.

Is he right? Let's begin with the last statement. It is clearly false. Dr. Francis Collins, the physician-scientist who led the human genome mapping project, was brought up in a home where religion was not taken seriously. He was an atheist until his doctoral studies and his experiences with dying patients led him to belief. He now sees God's handiwork in the magnificent complexity of life, as he explains in his book, *The Language of God*.

The list of intelligent former atheists who have become believers is long and impressive. They come from every field of science, philosophy, and academics: Dr. Allan Sandage, a renowned astronomer; Mortimer Adler, editor of the *Great Books of the Western World*; Dr. Diane Komp, MD, professor of pediatric oncology at

Yale University; Dr. Howard Storm, chairman of the art department at Northern Kentucky University; C. S. Lewis, one of the great authors and thinkers of the twentieth century; Lee Strobel, investigative journalist at the *Chicago Tribune*; Andre Frossard, a French journalist; Antony Flew, a champion of atheism for over fifty years; and...the list could go on indefinitely. But I'll just quote the humorous remark of an atheist teetering on the brink of belief, "I'm still an atheist, thank God."

There are many reasons why atheists become believers. Allan Sandage determined that there is nothing that causes the vast and beautiful universe to be. He reasoned that because it could not have come from nothing, there must be a Being outside the universe who gave it existence. Antony Flew was converted by recent scientific discoveries, especially the findings of DNA research. Mortimer Adler and Lee Strobel were drawn to God by philosophical reasoning and careful study. Diane Komp found God in the remarkable spiritual experiences of dying children. Others, like Howard Storm, Andre Frossard, and C. S. Lewis, encountered God as a Person who broke through their consciousness in ways that turned darkness to light, leaving them utterly convinced of the reality of God's existence.

Why do some atheists remain in unbelief? They make the fundamental error of claiming that the only real knowledge is that gained by scientific means. Atheists say, "If I can't measure God or examine God under a microscope, God cannot exist." But if God exists, he must transcend the material universe and be beyond measurement, or he cannot be God. Faith does not, and cannot, put God under a microscope. Faith is reasonable because it finds good cause to believe in God. Scientists become believers because they see magnificence and order in creation, and realize that it must come from God or it must come from nothing.

Because atheists cannot see God under a microscope, they claim God cannot exist. Therefore, they say, everything must come from nothing. But nothingness cannot be observed under a microscope either. Atheists must make a far more difficult leap of faith than those who believe in God, a leap from everything to nothing!

Many scientists find faith in God more reasonable. Allan Sandage says the world is too complicated to have been formed by accident: "I am convinced that the existence of life with all its order in each of its organisms is simply too well put together....This situation...becomes more astonishing every year as the scientific results become more detailed. Because of this, many scientists are now driven to faith by their very work" (www.leaderu.com/truth/1truth15.html).

KNOWING GOD THROUGH SCIENCE

If you want to know God, Saint Paul says, just look at the world. Everyone can find God, for, "Ever since the creation of the world his eternal power and divine nature, invisible though they are, have been understood and seen through the things he has made" (Romans 1: 20).

This was true in Paul's time. It is true today. And as science learns more about the nature of creation, it can help us achieve a better knowledge of God. Star-gazers of Paul's day probably numbered stars in the thousands; they knew God had to be great to create such a universe. Today's astronomers say that our Milky Way galaxy contains more than one hundred billion stars and that the universe contains more than one hundred billion galaxies. God IS great.

People have always marveled at the mystery of life, but now we are told things previous generations could hardly have imagined. The average adult human body, for example, contains about seventy-five trillion soft tissue cells. Each second, every one of these cells produces two thousand proteins from three hundred to one thousand combinations of amino acids. God likes vastness, and intricacy.

Such scientific findings have brought new meaning to Paul's words in the first chapter of Romans. Dr. Fritz Schaefer said,

"The significance and joy in my science comes in the occasional moments of discovering something new and saying to myself, 'So that's how God did it!'" (*U.S. News & World Report*, December 23, 1991). Science shows God to be greater than the ancients could have imagined.

THE MORAL LAW AND PHILOSOPHY

Another way people can come to know God is through the moral law, as C. S. Lewis argues in his book, *Mere Christianity*. Human beings agree that certain things, like torturing a baby for fun, are evil. On a personal level, most people (even atheists!) will say you should not walk into their house and take something that belongs to them. Such concepts of right and wrong imply a universal moral law that judges all people. It must come from mind, not from matter. Therefore, there must be a Mind above us all, namely God.

Dr. John Patrick, another former atheist, tells a story showing how people more readily admit the reality of objective right and wrong when it involves them. A student worked hard on an essay to prove that right and wrong are subjective. He did his research, wrote well, turned in the paper, and received a "C" as his grade. He was upset and went to argue with the teacher. The professor agreed that the paper was excellent, then added, "But I hate blue folders!" The student got the point, realizing that if right and wrong were indeed subjective, the professor could grade any way he wanted.

There are other philosophical arguments to demonstrate God's existence. Saint Thomas Aquinas offers five classical arguments from motion, causality, contingency, perfection, and design. These arguments may not seem as convincing to some people today as do the findings of science, but they can help us appreciate the careful reasoning that leads many to belief in God.

A modern philosopher who spent his lifetime studying the great thinkers of history, including Aquinas, was Mortimer Adler. Born in 1902, he considered himself a pagan as late as 1980, when he wrote *How to Think About God*, refining earlier arguments for God's existence. Soon afterward, he became a Christian, and in 2000 (at the age of 98!), a Roman Catholic.

Is there a God to be known? Yes, Paul proclaims, from the things God has made. Richard Dawkins may rail against believers, but more and more scientists are saying, "I'm no longer an atheist, thank God!"

QUESTIONS FOR DISCUSSION AND REFLECTION

Have you read books by any of the former atheists mentioned in this chapter or by any other former atheists? If so, what most impressed you about the reasons given for believing in God? Of the reasons in this chapter for believing in God, which do you find most persuasive? Why? What is the most important reason why people doubt God's existence? Which of the authors mentioned in the chapter could best address that issue?

ACTIVITIES

Spend time in prayer, meditating on Paul's words in Romans 1:20. Consider those aspects of creation that most inspire you to find and worship God. Check out the Web site referenced in this chapter. Do an Internet search on the names of former atheists mentioned in the text and learn more about their lives and writings.

CHAPTER 3

Believing in God or
Believing in Nothing

A devout Catholic, in a discussion with his atheist friend, said, "You have your reasons for believing in nothing. I have my reasons for believing in God. But if I am wrong, I'll never know it. If you are right, you'll never know it."

That's a humorous statement and true as far as it goes. But it doesn't go far enough. Believers cannot prove by scientific methods that God exists, and atheists cannot prove that there's nothing behind the universe. Science depends on what is measurable and observable. God cannot be measured or observed, or he would be just a limited part of our material universe. And, of course, "nothingness" cannot be measured or observed. We must believe in God or in nothing.

This is where the statement above falls short. It's true that if believers were mistaken in thinking there is a God who gives eternal life, death would be the end of everything. Believers would never know they were wrong. If atheists were right, death would end everything for them too. They'd never be able to turn to believers and say, "Ha, you see, we were right!"

But the statement doesn't go far enough. It implies that belief is like a coin toss. Call "heads" or "tails," flip the coin of life, and take your chances, with no good reason to choose one side or the other.

This is not the case. There is a big difference between believing in God and believing in nothing. While we cannot prove the existence of God by using scientific methods, we can show that it is more reasonable to believe in God than to believe in nothing. Why? First of all, believing in nothing demands a universal negative: "There is no God."

THE UNIVERSAL NEGATIVE

I can examine a tabletop and say with confidence, "There are no mice there." I could say there are no mice in a house, but I'd have to search carefully to be sure. Before I could deny the presence of mice in a city, I'd have to do a lot of investigating. The claim, "There is no God," would require far more searching. It means there is no evidence for God anywhere in the universe. That is a brash statement that can't be proven. But it's the best atheists can do.

As a matter of fact, that is how many atheists argue their position. They say, "If there is a God, why do innocent children suffer?" "If God planned the universe, why do things go wrong?" Atheists can only give reasons why they suppose there is no God. "There is," they argue, "no real evidence anywhere in the universe for belief. There never has been. There never will be." That's the universal negative. Atheists cannot say, "I'll prove to you that there is nothing. Here it is."

GOOD REASONS FOR BELIEF IN GOD

Those who believe in God, on the other hand, point to good reasons why there must be a God. We considered some of those in the last chapter: the discoveries of science, philosophical reasoning, the existence of right and wrong. Here I'd like to consider another important reason for belief in God: the experiences of people who have met God.

Some of these people have had every reason for NOT believing in God. Elie Wiesel, in his book, *Night*, describes how he, in 1944 at age fifteen, was arrested with his parents and three sisters, and then brought to Auschwitz. Elie watched his mother and youngest sister dragged to the gas chamber. He and his father were forced to work at hard labor under appalling conditions. His father died of starvation just a few months before the death camps were liberated.

Elie saw outrages beyond imagining: babies tossed into the air and used for target practice by German troops, women and children pushed alive into trenches filled with blazing gasoline, cruelties without number. Elie, a devout Jew, could not find God in such unspeakable misery. He describes his desolation: "I was the accuser, God the accused. My eyes had opened and I was alone, terribly alone in a world without God..." (*Night*, page 68).

But forty years later, Elie said at his Nobel Peace Prize Acceptance Speech in Oslo: "Blessed be Thou...for giving us life, for sustaining us, and for enabling us to reach this day.... I have faith. Faith in the God of Abraham, Isaac, and Jacob, and even in His creation. Without it no action would be possible" (*Night*, page 120).

I can understand how Elie could question God's existence in the horrors of the death camps. But I cannot understand how he could return to belief without a God to believe in. Elie experienced God. He turned from nothing to Someone he knew was real.

Those who deny God must not only reject the arguments for God's existence mentioned in Chapter 2. They must also dismiss people like Elie Wiesel. They must claim that he and others who say they have experienced God are either lying or deluded.

THEY HAVE MET HIM: GOD EXISTS

There are many believers who have experienced God, and they cover a wide spectrum. There are the children described by Doctor Diane Komp in her book, *Images of Grace*, children who brought her from atheism to belief. They were dying of cancer, but experienced God's love and the assurance of eternal life. They were for Doctor Komp a "window to heaven."

There is John Pridmore, a former hit man for a London gang, who had an encounter with God that turned his life around. Pridmore had gained wealth and power through his criminal interests, but one day he beat a man almost to death. At first he thought the victim was dead, and this shocked him into realizing how evil he had become. In a moment, he was overcome by God's presence and by Christ's grace and mercy. Abandoning his old life, he turned to Jesus. Over the past fifteen years he has spoken to hundreds of thousands, inviting them to find in Christ the life and love he had spurned until he was touched by God.

Dr. Howard Storm, a university professor and an atheist, says he once pitied believers. If they had his intelligence, he thought, they would be atheists, just like him. Then, as he explained on national television, he had a near-death experience while in Paris during which he left his body and went to hell. But doctors revived him, and he came back a believer. He KNEW his experience had been real. He said, "If it were not for God's mercy, I would be in hell forever."

Andre Frossard, a brilliant journalist, had an experience that turned him from atheism to belief in God. As he writes in his book, *I Have Met Him: God Exists*, Andre was a "perfect atheist," "the kind that no longer ever question their atheism" (page 24). Then, when his life without God seemed to be going quite well, he was astonished by a revelation of God's presence and truth that instantly turned him into a Catholic. Forty years later he remained certain that he had met God. Even the deaths of two beloved children could not make him doubt the reality of his experience.

Are all these people, from little children to highly intelligent adults, lying or deluded? "Yes," the atheist contends. "All these people are mistaken. I know what they've experienced more surely than they do." Such a claim, as implied in the title of Richard Dawkin's book, *The God Delusion*, is itself a delusion built on arrogance, not science.

Atheists can say, "We find no proof of God's existence. Therefore, what underlies physical reality is nothing. There is no meaning in life, no source of right and wrong, no reason to accept truth as truth, or falsehood as falsehood." Believers can say, "We have rational motives for belief in God. We have cause to trust those who've had a personal experience of God."

We who believe in God do have good reasons for faith. And in heaven, we'll know we are right. We'll all be able to say, with Andre Frossard, "I have met Him: God exists."

QUESTIONS FOR DISCUSSION AND REFLECTION

Many intelligent atheists have had such clear experiences of God that they became believers. Why do you think only some people have such experiences? Have you ever had such an experience? Discuss G. K. Chesterton's remark, "Atheism is indeed the most daring of all dogmas...for it is the assertion of a universal negative" (www.online-literature.com/chesterton/twelve-types/7/). What does he mean?

ACTIVITIES

Read Romans 1:16–32, where Paul describes the guilt of pagans who refuse to worship the true God. A college professor, Dr. J. Budziszewski, after turning from atheism to Catholicism, describes how he was guilty of ignoring God. Consider how his story echoes Paul:

Visualize a man opening up the access panels of his mind and pulling out all the components that have God's image stamped on them....I was that man. Because I pulled out more and more, there was less and less that I could think about. But because there was less and less that I could think about, I thought I was becoming more and more focused. Because I believed things that filled me with dread, I thought I was smarter and braver than the people who didn't believe them. I thought I saw an emptiness at the heart of the universe that was hidden from their foolish eyes. Of course I was the fool.

WWW.LEADERU.COM/REAL/RI9801/BUDZISZEWSKI.HTML

CHAPTER 4

Getting to Know God
Through Scripture

A little boy asked his grandfather, "Do you know how you and God are alike?" Grandpa mentally polished his halo and said, "No, how are we alike?" The child replied, "You're both old."

We know a lot more about God than his age! That's because God has revealed himself to us, above all in Sacred Scripture. As previous chapters have shown, we can, by using our intelligence, conclude that God exists. We arrive at this conclusion from the discoveries of science, philosophical reasoning, the existence of right and wrong, and the experiences of people who have met God. We learn much about God from creation: "The heavens are telling the glory of God; and the firmament proclaims his handiwork" (Psalm 19:1). But to really know who God is, we need the Bible.

SCRIPTURE: THE OLD TESTAMENT

Scripture records how God has revealed himself to humanity, how God has spoken to people, and how they have responded through the ages. The first part of Scripture, the Old Testament, was written and preserved by the Jewish people, who traced their ancestry back to Abraham, a tribal chieftain who lived about nineteen centuries before Christ. Abraham heard God speak, telling him to migrate to what is now Palestine. God had surely been speaking to human beings since creation, but few listened with the attention of Abraham. As a result, the Jewish people, looking back to Abraham and to other great leaders like Moses and David, began to keep a record of God's dealings with people. That record is now preserved in the forty-six books of the Old Testament.

In these books we discover the Jewish people's best impressions of God. We see that they learned of the one, true God. They believed that God created all things, including the first human beings. God created Adam and Eve "in his image" (Genesis 1:27), free, able to know and love. God intended that they find happiness through grace, God's life and love. Unfortunately, Adam and Eve misused their freedom, rejected God, and chose to look for happiness by putting themselves ahead of God.

As a result, we inherited from Adam and Eve a world "disgraced" by sin. We live in a world where sin so blinds us to God's presence that many people see creation without the Creator, and hear nature's voice without realizing that the music of birdsong and the thunder of storms speak the language of their Maker. An Old Testament writer asked, "...if they had the power to know so much that they could investigate the world, how did they fail to find sooner the Lord of these things?" (Wisdom 13:9). But fail they did, showing that we need the Bible to find the Lord, to know God as we should.

In the Old Testament we learn that God is Father, not in the sense that God is like human fathers, with limitations and weaknesses. Rather, since we are made in God's image and likeness, any good in human fathers is derived from God the Father. God loves us "with an everlasting love" (Jeremiah 31:3). God is holy (Isaiah 6:3), good (Psalm 73:1), and righteous (Psalm 11:7). God calls us to holiness (Leviticus 11:44), yet is "compassionate and merciful; he forgives sins and saves in time of distress" (Sirach 2:11).

God created humankind in his image. Because God made us male and female (Genesis 1:27), we can learn much about God from mothers. "As a mother comforts her child, so I will comfort you" (Isaiah 66:13). The Book of Sirach proclaims that God loves you "more than does your mother" (4:10).

SCRIPTURE: THE NEW TESTAMENT

We could not have known God's love and holiness without the revelation of the Old Testament. And the news about God was to get even better in the New Testament. For it is the Good News, the Gospel, of Jesus Christ, God's only Son.

Jesus revealed that God is not isolated power, but a loving Family. God is Father, Son, and Holy Spirit. God is Father because he knows himself from all eternity with knowledge so perfect that it is a Person, the Son. From all eternity, Father and Son love each other with a love so perfect that it is a Person, the Holy Spirit. This reality, that there are three Persons in one God, is the Trinity.

Followers of Christ have studied and discussed the Trinity ever since Jesus revealed it. Guided by the Holy Spirit, the Catholic Church learned to express the Trinity as three Persons in one divine Nature. Because in each human being there is only one person in one human nature, we cannot fully comprehend the Trinity. But we can, in our own limited way, get to know God as Father, Son, and Holy Spirit.

JESUS

The best way to know God is through Jesus. The New Testament says that the Second Person of the Trinity, the Son, called the "Word" in John's Gospel, became human. "In the beginning was the Word, and the Word was with God, and the Word was God.... And the Word became flesh and lived among us" (John 1:1, 14). Jesus is one divine Person with two natures, human and divine. Because Jesus is human, we can relate to him and understand his words and actions. Because he is God, everything about him reveals who God really is. Jesus is "the image of the invisible God" (Colossians 1:15).

If we want to know God, we should look to Jesus. The more we learn about him, the better we will know God. So we turn to the New Testament, especially the Gospels. We look also to the Church Jesus founded and to prayer, communication with Jesus.

If we are looking for a place to begin, we might consider Christmas, Good Friday, and Easter. These highlights of the Church year tell us much about God, and about God's attitudes toward us and our world.

CHRISTMAS, GOOD FRIDAY, AND EASTER

Our world is far from perfect. There are wars, terrorism, and crime. There are natural disasters, tornados, hurricanes, earthquakes, and drought. There are accidents, disease, and the afflictions of old age. And death looms over everything. Where is God in all of this?

Some people suppose that God made the universe and then left creation on its own. Others are overwhelmed by earth's problems and despair of ever finding God.

Christmas shows that God did not leave creation on its own, that God is present even in places as unlikely as a stable. Christmas proclaims that "God so loved the world that he gave his only Son" (John 3:16), and that God is as lovable as a tiny child held in the arms of his parents.

Good Friday testifies that God suffers with us. While there are no easy answers to earth's problems, we can be certain that God is not indifferent to our pain. There are times when we say with Jesus, "My God, my God, why have you forsaken me?" (Matthew 27:46). But God does not forsake us. God is someone we can trust as we pray with Jesus: "Father, into your hands I commend my spirit" (Luke 23:46).

Easter rings out the news that death is not an end. It is a new beginning. God has planted a longing in our hearts for something this life cannot supply. Easter assures us that God will supply it in eternal life. Our restless hearts will cease to be restless when they rest in God.

There is so much more to know about Jesus, and about the Father and Holy Spirit, and we will continue our study of the Trinity in the next chapter, "God Made Us to Know Him." Getting to know God is the privilege, the challenge, and the most exciting business of being human. The search should last a lifetime, and continue forever in heaven. Knowing God IS eternal life (John 17:3). For this, Jesus introduces us to God and tells us much more than his age!

QUESTIONS FOR DISCUSSION AND REFLECTION

Which of the Old Testament passages that describe God in this chapter is your favorite? Identify a passage in the New Testament that most helps you to know and love Jesus. In what ways does Jesus help us to know the Father? The Holy Spirit?

ACTIVITIES

In your own words, explain how Christmas, Good Friday, and Easter address the greatest problems we face as human beings. For a more thorough explanation of Catholic doctrine on the Trinity, read the *Catechism*, numbers 232–267. For a summary of the Good News, the Gospel, preached by Jesus, see my book, *"We Believe..." A Survey of the Catholic Faith* (Liguori Publications, pages 26–28). Meditate on these words of Saint Paul, and consider how all families on earth have their origin in the Family that is the Trinity: "For this reason I bow my knees before the Father, from whom every family in heaven and on earth takes its name" (Ephesians 3:14–15).

CHAPTER 5

Getting to Know God as Father, Son, and Holy Spirit

Roger lives alone on a 200-acre farm in Iowa. He has many limitations, mental and physical. Growing up as a child in the 1940s, Roger showed symptoms of what would now be called autism. After attempts at "book-learning" failed, Roger was taken out of school to stay home at the family farm. There he helped with simple jobs in the fields. When he was twenty-three years old, his shirt sleeve caught in a machine, and his arm was ripped off at the shoulder. After a long recuperation, Roger returned to the farm where he lived with his parents until their deaths. Then he was watched over by his sister, a nurse, for many years. Since she died, he has lived alone, under the care of his cousin, Ron, who from another state manages Roger's finances, health care, and the farm business. Roger's only companion on the farm is his beloved dog, Tippy. Roger talks to Tippy constantly and won't consider moving to a supervised care facility because he can't imagine life without his little friend.

Roger is now almost seventy years old, and Ron told me about his concerns for Roger's spiritual condition. Roger was baptized as a child but doesn't seem able to understand the concept of God's presence or of life after death. "I'd like to talk to him about God, about heaven, but I'm not sure where to begin," said Ron. I suggested that he might try telling Roger about Jesus and that he might begin with Tippy. Something like this:

"You know how much Tippy loves you, Roger? And how much

you love him? How he's always at your side and how you can talk to him about everything? Well, Jesus is your best friend, your Lord and God. He is always at your side. You can talk to him anytime, about anything. And when God calls you home, Jesus will be there to welcome you to new life where there will be no more suffering or pain, and where every tear will be wiped away."

It might seem irreverent to use an animal as a pattern to talk about Jesus. But the Bible does just that. Jesus is the "Lamb of God" (John 1:29) and the "Lion of the tribe of Judah" (Revelation 5:5). A beloved dog certainly could stand as a symbol of Christ's unconditional love for Roger, who because of his limitations, might otherwise feel alone and unloved.

We must not complicate our efforts to know God. It is true that God is a Trinity of Persons: Father, Son, and Holy Spirit. It is true that we can no more understand the Trinity than a daisy can understand Einstein. But we can and should get to know the Father, Son, and Holy Spirit. How? Jesus tells us that we must accept the kingdom of God like a little child (Luke 18:17). We can know the Father and Holy Spirit by getting to know Jesus, and getting to know Jesus can be as simple as enjoying the embrace of his love, letting him take us in his arms and bless us, as he blessed the little children (Mark 10:13–16).

KNOWING JESUS

Getting to know Jesus begins with reading the Gospels. There we see that Jesus was a down-to-earth human being. Raised in a small town, he seemed such a normal child that when he came back as a miracle worker, people refused to believe he was special (Mark 6:1–6). Jesus' parables show that he loved nature and celebrated life: the sun and rain, wild flowers and vines and trees, moths and birds and foxes, people building houses, farmers planting crops, women baking bread, and fishermen casting nets (Matthew 5–7; 13).

Jesus liked people and people liked him. He was always getting invited to meals (Luke 4:39; 7:36; 10:38; 14:1). He was friendly and outgoing and enjoyed being with others (John 1:35–51). He went to parties and even worked a miracle to keep a party going (John 2:1–11). He noticed people whom others missed (Mark 10:46–52). To him elderly widows and despised sinners were important (Mark 12:41–44; Mark 14:3–9).

Jesus was merciful and compassionate. He defended a woman accused of adultery (John 8:1–11). He shed tears at the death of Lazarus (John 11). He wept over the fate of Jerusalem (Luke 19:41–44).

Jesus mightily opposed evil. He drove from the temple those who turned God's house into a market (John 2:13–16). He refused to compromise when doctrinal issues were at stake and let unbelievers walk away (John 6:60–67). He told sinners to reform (John 8:11). He chastised cynics and hypocrites, threatening them with the fire of hell (Matthew 23:23–33).

Jesus was brave, yet felt distress and sorrow (Mark 14:32–42). He was born like us and chose to accept an awful death for love of us (Luke 2:1–7; Luke 23).

Jesus is a friend. "No one has greater love than this, to lay down one's life for one's friends. You are my friends" (John 15:13–14).

KNOWING THE FATHER

If you know Jesus, you know the Father. At the Last Supper, Jesus said, "If you know me, you will know my Father also." Philip replied, "Lord, show us the Father, and we will be satisfied." Then Jesus said, "Whoever has seen me has seen the Father" (see John 14:7–9). The wonderful attributes of Jesus are those of his Father as well.

Jesus told parables that paint a marvelous portrait of the Father. The parable of the prodigal son demonstrates the Father's mercy: the Father is more eager to forgive us than we are to be forgiven (Luke 15:11–35). Jesus' parable of the unforgiving servant speaks of God's righteousness and shows we must let God's mercy shine in our lives (Matthew 18:23–35). Jesus assures us that the Father wants us to be in his company forever: "In my Father's house there are many dwelling places. I have prepared one for you, and I will take you there" (John 14:2–3).

KNOWING THE HOLY SPIRIT

Knowing Jesus brings knowledge also of the Holy Spirit. The Spirit is love, not in an abstract sense, but "God who loves." Jesus calls the Holy Spirit our Advocate, our Helper who speaks to us (John 14:16; 16:7–14). The Holy Spirit brings the power of the wind and fire which strengthened the Apostles at Pentecost (Acts 2:1–4). "Likewise the Spirit helps us in our weakness" (Romans 8:26). The Spirit lives in us as a friend: "And I will ask the Father, and he will give you another Advocate, to be with you forever. This is the Spirit of truth, whom the world cannot receive, because it neither sees him nor knows him. You know him, because he abides with you, and he will be in you" (John 14:16–17).

OUR KNOWLEDGE OF GOD

Jesus wants us to know him and the Father and Holy Spirit as our best friends. We must get to know God in a personal way. Reading the Bible can teach us much about God. But until we realize that God is as close to us as the air, we don't know enough about God. "In God we live and move and have our being" (Acts 17:28).

Until we realize that God loves us unconditionally, as a loyal dog loves his master (but multiplied by billions!), we don't know enough about God. That's why Roger's story helped me think and pray more about how God loves me. And I hope it gives you a new insight into God's love for you.

For God wants us to know, love, and serve him in this world so that we can be happy with him in the next. I think Roger can help us appreciate the next world too...

WHERE EVERY TEAR WILL BE WIPED AWAY

When the time comes for Roger to go home, when he stands before gates that offer access to a destination of awesome beauty, Jesus will be there, smiling, arms open in welcome. Roger, with a mind now perfectly clear, will see Jesus, his friend, his Savior, his Lord and God. And there, I am sure, next to Jesus, will be Tippy.

Tippy will rush, tail wagging furiously, into Roger's arms. Jesus will wait quietly for a moment, still smiling, and then say to Roger, "In my Father's house are many dwelling places. Let me show you yours." Roger will respond, "Now I will see the Father, and that will be enough."

QUESTIONS FOR DISCUSSION AND REFLECTION

Do you know people like Roger, dealing with mental and physical handicaps, yet dearly loved by God? In spite of such handicaps, how might they be more spiritually advanced than the rest of us? Have you ever considered the love of dogs (and other pets) for their owners as no accident, but designed by God as a sign of his unconditional love for us? Review the sections in this chapter that describe each Divine Person. Decide which quality for each Divine Person most touches you.

ACTIVITIES

Place yourself in God's presence, in whom "we live and move and have our being." Listen as the Father tells you, "I have loved you with an everlasting love" (Jeremiah 31:3). Look into the eyes of Jesus as he says "You are my friend" (John 15:14). Jesus calls the Holy Spirit our Advocate, our Helper who speaks to us (John 14:16; 16:7–14). Become aware of the Spirit's presence within you, and ask the Holy Spirit to speak to your heart.

CHAPTER 6

God Made You to Love Him

"I'm excited about dying," said eight-year-old Brooke, "because then I'll get to be with Jesus and Grandpa Ron." Brooke had battled brain cancer for over a year, and she was dying. But Jesus came and assured her of his love for her. Fear of death was pushed to the background by Jesus' love for Brooke and by her love for Jesus.

Jesus loves little children. In New Testament times, he took them in his arms and blessed them (Mark 10:16). He embraces them with his love today, sometimes in miraculous ways, as little Brooke discovered. And Jesus loves us all, with a love that is more than miraculous.

We began this discussion on the purpose of life with the question from the *Baltimore Catechism*, "Why did God make you?" We've been reflecting on the answer, "God made me to know him, to love him, and to serve him in this world, and to be happy with him forever in heaven." So far, we've considered how we KNOW God. Now we turn to how we LOVE God.

But why begin with Jesus' love for Brooke and for us? We take this approach because before we consider our love for God, we must examine God's love for us.

GOD LOVES US FIRST

The New Testament proclaims: "In this is love, not that we loved God but that he loved us" (1 John 4:10). "We love because he first loved us" (1 John 4:19). We might mistakenly think that God will love us if we love him enough or if we are good enough to earn his love. No. God loves us first, and only his love can make it possible for us to love in return.

There are many reasons why this is so. You may have heard the statement that our bodies are made of stardust. The matter in our solar system was formed out of dust and gas from stars that exploded billions of years ago. But where did those long-dead stars come from? Great scientists like Dr. Allan Sandage say that they came from God. The material universe cannot have caused itself or come from nothing. It was created by an all-wise, all-powerful Being who exists outside the limits of space and time. Albert Einstein in his famous equation, $E = mc2$ (energy equals mass times the speed of light squared), shows that all matter could come from energy. Everything in our universe, including us, came from God, who is infinite energy and wisdom. We would not exist if God had not existed from all eternity.

God did not make us as he made rocks or trees or animals. God made us "in his image" (Genesis 1:27), capable of knowledge and love. We are able to love only because God gives us the ability to love.

Further, while our bodies are composed of stardust that is billions of years old, our souls are individually created by God. We are who we are because God called us into being as persons. Your parents didn't know what they were getting, but God did! In Jeremiah 1:5, God says, "Before I formed you in the womb, I knew you." God wanted YOU because he knew and loved you from all eternity so that you could know and love God and others as well.

HOW MUCH DOES GOD LOVE US?

For an answer to this question, let's begin with Jesus. Someone has remarked: "I asked Jesus how much he loves me. And he stretched out his arms on the cross and said, 'This much.'" God so loved the world that he gave us his Son (John 3:16), and Jesus loves us so much he gave his life for us.

These truths can be expressed so often that they cease to have real impact. Some years ago, they took on a special meaning for me when a mother told me about the birth of her youngest child. Several months into the pregnancy, she was diagnosed with cancer. Doctors advised a treatment that would have killed the child. She told them she would wait until after the child was born, even though this would place her life in danger. She delivered a healthy boy and then was treated for the cancer. After her recovery, she said that she would gladly have given her own life if that's what it took to save her child. She spoke in a matter-of-fact way that left me amazed. Later I reflected that Jesus must have spoken the words in John 15:13 in the same matter-of-fact way: "Certainly I'll give my life for my friends. What else would you expect?" That's how Jesus loves us. We must never take such love for granted.

Another way of learning to appreciate God's love for us is suggested by Saint Paul. He teaches that God's divine nature is made known to us "through the things he has made" (Romans 1:20). If we study what astronomy and science have discovered about the things God has made, we can't help but be astonished. As mentioned earlier, God has made a universe of one hundred billion galaxies. No human being can create a single galaxy. This fact gives us a way of estimating God's greatness and love, for it shows that God is more than one hundred billion times as great as any human being. "God is love" (1 John 4:16), and this means that God loves us more than one hundred billion times as much as any human being could.

Think of the person who loves you most. Multiply that love by one hundred billion. This will give you some idea of how much God loves you. It should help explain why God would become a little child at Bethlehem to show us how to live. It should help explain why God would be willing to die on the cross for us if that's what it took to free us from the clutches of sin and death. "...he humbled himself and became obedient to the point of death—even death on a cross" (Philippians 2:7).

GOD'S LOVE IN A TROUBLED WORLD

"That's well and good," one might say. "But why do I have so many problems? Why is the world such a mess? If God loves us, why doesn't he do something to make the world better?"

Such thoughts can rise up from time to time and cause us to question God's love. If they do, we need to consider the love good parents have for their children. Good parents love their children unconditionally. They do their best to teach and guide the children toward the moral choices that will bring true happiness. But parents can't force their children to love and can't force them to always do the right thing.

Because of human freedom, children can ignore parents, reject their love, and make choices that block that love. Children can make bad decisions and wander down pathways that lead to misery and pain. Many times in the course of my priestly ministry, I've sat with parents who wept over the self-destructive choices made by their children. The parents don't stop loving, but they grieve because their love is spurned and their counsel ignored.

This must be how a loving God feels about his children when they refuse to accept his love, when by sin and stupidity they bring grief on themselves and others. God does everything that love can do, and this can lead to tears, even for God. Jesus wept over Jerusalem and agonized: "If you, even you, had only recognized on this day the things that make for peace!" (Luke 19:41–42). When pain afflicts us in this troubled world, it is no reason to doubt God's love for us. It is rather reason to draw closer to a loving Christ who weeps for us and with us.

LOVE'S FINAL PLAN

Brooke spent her last days on earth with Jesus. Then Jesus welcomed her to new life, where she is happy with God forever. Jesus invites us to reflect on God's love, which makes it possible for us to love. Jesus wants to assure us, as he assured Brooke, that love can take away all fear. He wants us, like Brooke, to be excited at the prospect of being happy with God forever.

QUESTIONS FOR DISCUSSION AND REFLECTION

How can we be made of stardust if we are given life by God? Do you think that it is an exaggeration to say that God loves us more than one hundred billion times as much as any human being could love us? Why or why not? Do you know any parents who have risked their lives for their children? Do you think God can grieve at our sinfulness? How? Do you know parents who love their children and yet are hurt by the bad choices the children make? If God has the power to force us to do the right thing, why doesn't God use this power?

ACTIVITIES

Meditate on the death of Jesus on the cross as his greatest sign of love and friendship toward you. Thank Jesus for dying for you. Consider Saint Paul's statement that God's divine nature is made known to us "through the things he has made" (Romans 1:20). Go to the NASA Web site (www.nasa.gov) to find images of the universe taken by the Hubble space telescope. Ask God to help you see his handiwork in the marvels of creation. Think about those aspects of creation which most display God's goodness and beauty to you. Thank God for them.

CHAPTER 7

Loving God

B lessed Teresa of Calcutta, Mother Teresa, was known for her joyful love of God and others. A collection of her correspondence entitled, *Mother Teresa: Come Be My Light*, revealed that much of her life was devoid of spiritual consolation. *Time* Magazine placed her on its cover (September 3, 2007) with this heading: "The Secret Life of Mother Teresa—Her letters reveal a 50-year crisis of faith in which she rarely sensed the presence of God in her life."

Many people have been puzzled by such reports. How could such a saintly woman have a "crisis of faith"?

First, it is incorrect to call what Mother Teresa experienced a "crisis of faith." She surely felt spiritual darkness and dryness, apparently for a good part of her life. But this does not mean she lacked faith. Faith is not composed of feelings. Faith is the decision to put God first, to believe the words of Jesus, and to live according to his Gospel. "Faith is the assurance of things hoped for, the conviction of things not seen" (Hebrews 11:1). True faith can exist without feelings of joy and consolation.

Second, Mother Teresa may not have had ecstatic visions, but she did sense the presence of God in the poor. She saw Christ in them. She believed that whatever she did for others, she did for Christ. And her life shows how faith can lead to love.

LOVE IS A DECISION

In Chapter 6, we looked at God's great love for us and saw that we are capable of love only because God loves us first. "We love because he first loved us" (1 John 4:19). God's love empowers us to love God in return and to love others. But love, like faith, is more of a decision than an emotion. Mother Teresa showed this by her dedication to Jesus and her loving service of the poor. The more we learn how infrequently she felt God's love, the more we can admire the strength of her faith and love.

"Love is a decision" is an oft repeated phrase in the Marriage Encounter movement, with good reason. Love based on feelings does not last, as Hollywood news releases confirm again and again. Real love lasts because it is a decision. This is true of our love for God as well as our love for other people. Mother Teresa's love for God and neighbor shines out because she was faithful in her love commitments, to the time of her death.

LOVE OF GOD AND LOVE OF NEIGHBOR

Mother Teresa's life was a powerful witness to another fact about true love of God. Love of God finds expression in love of the neighbor. Scripture says:

> *Beloved, since God loved us so much, we also ought to love one another....Those who say, "I love God," and hate their brothers or sisters, are liars; for those who do not love a brother or sister whom they have seen, cannot love God whom they have not seen. The commandment we have from him is this: those who love God must love their brothers and sisters also.*
>
> 1 JOHN 4:11, 20–21

There is comfort in this passage. At times we might wonder whether we truly love God. How does a creature love the Creator? What if I don't have warm, fuzzy feelings about God?

If you don't, that's OK. If you love your neighbor, you love God. And if you don't have warm, fuzzy feelings about your neighbor, that's OK, too. Love is more a decision than a feeling. More accurately, love is a series of decisions to do what is best for the neighbor because God loves us. Scripture says: "If a brother or sister is naked and lacks daily food, and one of you says to them, 'Go in peace; keep warm and eat your fill,' and yet you do not supply their bodily needs, what is the good of that?" (James 2:15–16). Love is faith in action.

LOVE OF NEIGHBOR AND LOVE OF GOD

But we need guidance in determining what is best for the neighbor. In today's world, evil crimes like abortion and euthanasia are disguised as acts of love. Many who kill innocent babies say they do it because they "love" the mother of the unborn child. Many who want to kill the elderly say that they "love" the elderly and want them to avoid suffering and to "die with dignity." Love has been used to justify slavery and to mask many other kinds of wickedness. How can we know where real love leads?

An answer is given in the First Letter of Saint John. After saying that our love of God is genuine when we love our neighbor, John adds: "By this we know that we love the children of God, when we love God and obey his commandments" (1 John 5:2). God's commandments show us how to love our neighbor. If we break God's commandments, we cannot claim to love our neighbor, or God.

Abortion and euthanasia cannot be acts of love because they break God's commandment, "You shall not kill." God's commandments, interpreted and explained by the Church that Jesus founded, provide a blueprint for love of God and neighbor. We will see in future chapters that they teach us how to serve God. But first we will examine the meaning of love of God and will look at ways to grow in our love of God.

LOVE OF GOD AND FRIENDSHIP WITH GOD

For many people, love of God can seem abstract and otherworldly, out of the reach of ordinary individuals. But all true human love has its origin in God. So God's love for us and our love for God are as down-to-earth as a mother's love for her baby, as the tender caring of committed spouses, as the bond between good friends who would be willing to sacrifice life itself for the other.

In particular, the concept of friendship is worth considering. I've heard people say that we mustn't call God our friend because this would be arrogant. Well, it would be far more arrogant to contradict God! God calls us friends, and who are we to contradict God? In the Old Testament we read that God considered Moses as a friend. "Thus the Lord used to speak to Moses face-to-face, as one speaks to a friend" (Exodus 33:11).

Recall that Jesus said to the Apostles and to us, "I call you my friends" (John 15:14). Since Jesus is one with the Father and Holy Spirit, he calls us to friendship with the Trinity. Jesus says that the Father loves us as he loves Jesus (John 17:23). The Holy Spirit is "God who loves us."

The longer I live, the more I am convinced that friendship with God must be at the heart of everything we do. When we pray, especially when we attend Mass and receive Holy Communion, we should intend to strengthen our friendship with Jesus, the Father, and the Holy Spirit. In everything we do, we can work towards an ever-deepening friendship with God.

MOTHER TERESA'S FAITH AND LOVE

We shouldn't be surprised that Mother Teresa experienced dark feelings and desolation. She prayed constantly to share in Christ's sufferings. Her prayer was heard, and she experienced his desolation on the cross (Mark 15:34). But she never lost her sense of humor. In 1996 she told Prince Michael of Greece, "The other day I dreamed that I was at the gates of heaven. And Saint Peter said, 'Go back to Earth. There are no slums up here'" (*USA Today*, http://www. usatoday.com/news/mothert/mother01.htm).

On September 5, 1997, however, God called her home to stay. She had known, loved, and served God on earth. It was time for her to leave the slums and be happy forever in heaven.

QUESTIONS FOR DISCUSSION AND REFLECTION

Were you surprised by news reports of Mother Teresa's spiritual dryness and darkness? Have you ever experienced such dryness? Did it help you appreciate your need for God? In your opinion, is love more emotion or more decision? Do the media treat love primarily as an emotion or as a decision? If you were asked for a list of your five best friends, where would Jesus be on the list?

ACTIVITIES

This chapter mentions the spiritual darkness experienced by Mother Teresa. You may read a brief explanation of such darkness (often called the dark night of the soul) in the lives of saints at this web site: http://en.wikipedia.org/wiki/Dark_Night_of_the_Soul. Meditate for a few minutes on the Bible passages cited in this chapter, especially 1 John 4:11, 20–21.

CHAPTER 8

Growing in Love of God

While at a parish mission in Saint Louis, I celebrated Mass for the school children. After reading the Gospel, in which Jesus stated the two great commandments, I asked the older children, "What is the first and greatest commandment?" An eighth grader quickly replied, "You shall love the Lord your God." "Right," I said, turning to the smaller children with the question, "And the second greatest commandment is to love your...?" A first grade girl answered without hesitation: "Grandma!"

I couldn't argue with that. What Jesus actually said was: "The first is '...you shall love the Lord your God with all your heart, and with all your soul, and with all your mind, and with all your strength.' The second is this, 'You shall love your neighbor as yourself'" (Mark 12:30–31). But grandmas certainly fit into the second category, and, as we shall see, we can learn a lot about loving God from the way children love their grandmas.

WHY A COMMANDMENT TO LOVE GOD?

Why does Jesus command us to love God? Children don't need a commandment to love their grandmas, and no grandma needs to be ordered to love her grandchildren.

In a perfect world, we wouldn't need the first and greatest commandment, but our world is far from perfect. It is tainted by sin, and we can too easily concentrate on the material and miss the spiritual. Yet, material things decay and pass away. Spiritual realities, above all, God and God's love, endure forever.

Jesus emphasizes this in the first commandment. If we miss the love of God, we miss the main reason for being alive. We are alive to "know, love, and serve God," and in this we find the happiness we seek.

In Chapter 7, we saw that love is a matter more of decision than of feeling. So we can grow in love for God by making the right decisions. Loving God brings joy. Loving God more will bring more joy. How can we grow in our love for God?

MAKING THE RIGHT DECISIONS

The first step toward growing in God's love is reviewing the fact that God loves us first. Babies learn to love when they are loved by parents, grandparents, and family. We can grow in our love for God when we become more aware of God's love for us.

We must remember that we need love because we are made in the image and likeness of God. God is not an impersonal power plant on the edge of the universe. God is a Trinity of Persons—Father, Son, and Holy Spirit—who want to draw us into their community of love forever. Love cannot be forced, so God simply loves us and invites us to love in return. But it is easy to underestimate God's love. One way to overcome this tendency is to look at each Person in turn.

We may think of God the Father as Creator and remember, as we saw in Chapter 6, that the vastness of the universe indicates how God's love for us is more than one hundred billion times greater than that of any human being. The Father loves us infinitely more than could any human being, even Grandma! When talking to children, I ask them to think about how much their grandma loves them, and to multiply this by one hundred billion. This can help us appreciate the Father's words: "I have loved you with an everlasting love" (Jeremiah 31:3).

To appreciate Jesus' love for us, we need only look at a crucifix. Then we should hear Jesus say: "No one has greater love than this, to lay down one's life for one's friends" (John 15:13). Jesus loved us so much that he died for us.

As for the love of the Holy Spirit, we ought to realize that each of us is called to be a "dwelling place" of the Holy Spirit. "And I will ask the Father, and he will give you another Advocate, to be with you forever. This is the Spirit of truth....You know him, because he abides with you, and he will be in you" (John 14:16–17). We like to be close to those we love. The Holy Spirit loves us so much that he wants to live in us. Any time we choose, we can turn to this Guest of our souls, bask in his closeness, and enjoy his love and assistance.

THE THREE-MINUTE TRINITY PRAYER

Once we are convinced of God's love for us, we need practical, down-to-earth ways of staying in touch with the Father, Son, and Holy Spirit. One of my favorites is the "Three-minute Trinity Prayer." This prayer can help us stay close to the Trinity and grow in love of God.

Begin the first minute by adoring Father, Son, and Holy Spirit with the Sign of the Cross and Glory Be. Then think about the greatest blessing you've received in the past twenty-four hours, and thank God the Father for it. In the second minute, turn to Jesus, remember your most serious sin of the past twenty-four hours, and ask Jesus to forgive you. In the third, look ahead to the greatest challenge facing you in the next twenty-four hours and ask the Holy Spirit to help you face that challenge.

LIVING IN JESUS

The most powerful way to grow in love of God and intimacy with Jesus is the Mass, the Eucharist. Jesus tells us: "Those who eat my flesh and drink my blood live in me and I in them" (John 6:56). The physical and spiritual dimensions of our being interact powerfully with each other. A mother can express her love for her baby with an embrace, and the very act of holding her child strengthens her love. Jesus knows this, and so he gave us the Eucharist as a real, physical sign of his presence. At Communion time, we are physically, sacramentally, united to Jesus. He lives in us, and we in him.

Every time we attend Mass, we should look at the crucifix near the altar and see there the evidence of Christ's love. We should note each mention of his love in the readings and prayers. Above all, when we receive Jesus in Holy Communion, we should consider his love for us. We should gratefully profess our love for him, and ask him to help us grow in love.

EUCHARISTIC ADORATION

In the past few years, many parishes have instituted Eucharistic adoration, with exposition of the Blessed Sacrament at specific times or every hour every day. Such devotion to Jesus has brought great blessings to individuals and to entire parishes. Whether the Blessed Sacrament is exposed or not, Jesus remains available to us in every Catholic Church. An hour in the presence of Jesus can be a wonderful opportunity to grow in love of God.

What might we do during this hour of prayer? We can just enjoy being with Jesus, as with any friend. We can talk about family, work, and anything happening in our lives. We may reflect upon Scripture, read from a good spiritual book, pray the rosary, or use prayers from a favorite prayer book. Those who get into the habit of making an hour of adoration in the presence of Jesus find that the time goes by too quickly, just as it does in the presence of any good friend.

"Love Your Grandma"

The love of grandparents and grandchildren for one another is one of life's most precious gifts. Multiply that love by more than one hundred billion and you are on the way to glimpsing God's love for you. I need to spend more time reflecting on God's love. Perhaps you do, too.

After all, the first and greatest commandment is: "Love the Lord your God with all your heart, mind, soul, and strength."

Questions for Discussion and Reflection

Have you ever spent time considering how much God loves you? Does God love people even when they sin? If so, how can sin separate us from God's love? Do you experience the Mass as a physical bond of unity between you and Jesus? Why, or why not? Have you ever spent an hour in the presence of the Blessed Sacrament?

Activities

Quietly place yourself in God's presence, and pray the Three-minute Trinity Prayer. Commit these three Scripture verses to memory: "I have loved you with an everlasting love" (Jeremiah 31:3). "As the Father has loved me, so I have loved you: abide in my love" (John 15:9). "[The Holy Spirit] abides with you, and he will be in you" (John 14:17).

CHAPTER 9

God's Love in All Times and Places

It was Sunday morning, and the family was driving home from 9:00 Mass in St. Louis, Missouri. Grandma and Grandpa had come to visit and had attended grandson D.J.'s First Holy Communion a week earlier. They were in the car with D.J., his two sisters, and his mom and dad. The grandparents wanted to do a little sightseeing. There was much discussion as to where the family should go. Being avid gardeners, Mom and Grandma wanted to go to the Missouri Botanical Garden. The children wanted to go to the St. Louis Zoo. Mom tried to convince them that the Botanical Garden would be just as much fun. The discussion went back and forth, but D.J. remained adamant about going to the zoo. Mom reminded D.J. that he had just received his second Holy Communion. She told him to remember that Jesus was now living in his heart, and so he shouldn't be so stubborn about wanting to visit the zoo.

A few quiet minutes passed, and then from the back seat, D.J. calmly said, "Mom? Jesus wants to go to the zoo too!"

LIVING IN GOD'S LOVE

D.J.'s dad, Jim, told me this story at a parish mission. When I stopped laughing, I realized that there is an important lesson here. Jesus comes to us in Holy Communion, not just to be with us for a few minutes in church, but to go everywhere with us, even to the zoo.

We've been reflecting on the fact that God made us to love him. We saw in Chapter 8 that the most powerful way to grow in love of God and intimacy with Jesus is the Mass, the Eucharist. At the Mass we receive Jesus himself in Holy Communion. Jesus tells us: "Those who eat my flesh and drink my blood abide in me and I in them" (John 6:56). When we receive Holy Communion, we are as close to God as is possible in this life. Another special time of closeness is when we worship Jesus at eucharistic adoration. But as D.J. would tell us, Jesus wants to go to the zoo with us. Jesus would also want to go to the Botanical Garden or to any place we happen to be. How can we learn to be more conscious of Jesus' presence and love?

SPIRITUAL COMMUNION

One way is the practice of spiritual communion, dear to the hearts of great Catholics like Saint Francis de Sales and Saint Faustina. Spiritual communion is an act of the mind and will whereby we invite Jesus to live in our heart when we cannot receive him sacramentally. We can do this anytime or anywhere with a short prayer like this: "Jesus, I can't receive you now in Holy Communion, but I invite you to come into my heart. Live in me and help me to think, speak, and act like you. Amen."

A spiritual communion can take as long as we wish, even an entire hour of prayer in an adoration chapel, in a quiet room at home, or in the beauty of God's great outdoors. Many years ago, when I was pastor at St. Denis Parish in Benton, Missouri, I taught the smaller children a method of prayer that is a form of spiritual communion. It's a method that works well for adults too, and I still use it today.

This method is based on Jesus' words: "Listen! I am standing at the door, knocking; if you hear my voice and open the door, I will come in to you and eat with you, and you with me"(Revelation 3:20). First, imagine a special house of prayer. Build it any way you like, and place it anywhere in the world you want. (My own house of prayer is in the mountains, with a wall of glass that overlooks a small lake framed by snow covered peaks.) Your house of prayer can be on the beach, in a forest, on a sunny meadow, on the bank of a river or stream. In this house, have a room with two chairs. When it's time for your spiritual communion, enter that room, sit in one of the chairs, and relax for a few moments, remembering the words of Jesus, "Peace I leave with you; my peace I give to you" (John 14:27). Next, pay attention to your breathing. If it is shallow, deepen it. If it is rapid, slow it down. Reflect on this verse of Scripture: "The spirit of God has made me, and the breath of the Almighty gives me life" (Job 33:4).

Then, hear a knock at the door. Rise, go to the door, and open it to welcome Jesus. Embrace him, and feel his strong arms holding you close to his heart. Take him to the chair opposite yours, invite him to make himself comfortable, and then sit down facing him. Notice how attentive he is to your every gesture of hospitality, how his love for you shines in his eyes and in his smile. He looks at you and asks, "What would you like to talk about?"

You may talk to Jesus about anything you want. If you are happy about recent events, discuss them with Jesus. If you are upset, talk about your anger or your fears. If you are worried about the health of a relative, a job situation, or anything else, talk about it with Jesus. Jesus listens carefully to every word. Then sit quietly and hear his reply. It might be words he uses in Scripture like, "I will be with you always" (Matthew 28:20), or "If you love me, you will keep my word, and my Father will love you, and we will come to you and make our home with you" (see John 14:23). Or Jesus might address you in other words spoken to your heart.

After you and Jesus finish your conversation, walk with him to the door of your room and tell him goodbye. Invite him to come again. Embrace him, and tell him how much you are looking forward to his next visit, and to the next time you'll receive him sacramentally in Holy Communion. Then follow him from your house of prayer and return to your everyday activities.

Such spiritual communions are not the equivalent of Holy Communion, which is Christ's greatest Gift to us. But they can help us treasure our last reception of Jesus in Communion and look forward to the next. While we can't receive Jesus sacramentally many times a day, we can receive him spiritually as often as we want. Each spiritual communion is an opportunity to live in Christ and let Christ live in us, helping us grow in love.

ENJOYING JESUS' LOVE FOREVER

Jesus is always near, ready to share the events of life. But he is especially close in time of trouble. His passion and death show that he did not use his divine power to avoid pain. Instead, he endured ghastly suffering and a terrible death. He knows our afflictions and shares them with us. When we must carry a cross, Jesus gives us his strength, comfort, and peace. He promises, "Come to me, all you that are weary and are carrying heavy burdens, and I will give you rest" (Matthew 11:28).

When my younger brother Joe was diagnosed with inoperable lung cancer, I was devastated by the news, as he was, along with his whole family. It was a time to hear Jesus say, "Come to me." It was a time to learn how fragile this life can be, to realize that we are made for eternity. God made us to be happy forever, but rising to eternal life comes only after dying to this one.

If we let Jesus into the home of our hearts here on earth, if we welcome him into our prayer room when he stands at the door and knocks, then Jesus will welcome us into another room. "In my Father's house are many dwelling places....I will come again and will take you to myself, that where I am, there you may be also" (John 14:2–3). Six weeks after my brother received the diagnosis of cancer, he was called to his eternal dwelling place. I trust that Jesus was there to welcome Joe to the place prepared for him.

ZOOS, GARDENS, AND PARADISE

D.J.'s family went to the Botanical Garden. His mom promised him that he'd enjoy the Garden almost as much as the zoo. I'm not sure if D.J. found trees and flowers as exciting as lions and tigers. But I know one thing. Jesus went with him. And Jesus will go with us, anywhere, if only we invite him to come along.

QUESTIONS FOR DISCUSSION AND REFLECTION

Have you ever thought about Jesus joining you at the zoo or at your favorite recreational activity? How would you describe spiritual communion in your own words? Have you ever used a prayer like the "house of prayer" method? How do you allow Jesus to share all the events of your life, especially times of pain and suffering?

ACTIVITIES

Build a house of prayer for yourself and invite Jesus into your prayer room. Speak to him about what is on your mind, and listen as he responds. If you need architectural advice for your house of prayer, consider this passage by Saint John Chrysostom, Bishop of Constantinople, 347–407 AD:

Practice prayer from the beginning. Paint your house with the colors of modesty and humility. Make it radiant with the light of justice. Decorate it with the finest gold leaf of good deeds. Adorn it with the walls and stones of truth and generosity. Crown it with the pinnacle of prayer. In this way you will make it a perfect dwelling place for the Lord. You will be able to receive him as in a splendid palace, and through his grace you will already possess him, his image enthroned in the temple of your spirit.

OFFICE OF READINGS, FRIDAY AFTER ASH WEDNESDAY

CHAPTER 10

God's Love and Friendship

Some time ago, I called my doctor's office. When the reception-
ist answered, I gave her my name and told her I'd like to make
an appointment for my annual physical. She tapped a few keys on
her computer and then said with a note of uncertainty in her voice,
"Did you say your name was Father Oscar Lukefahr?" "Yes," I
replied. She hesitated, then asked, "Your date of birth?" I gave it.
She paused. Then she announced, "We have you listed as deceased."
"In that case," I said, "We won't need to schedule the physical."

We both laughed, then set a time for my appointment. But
afterward I sat at my desk and thought: Maybe this is how you
discover that you're really dead. At first you don't know you're gone.
Then people hesitate while talking to you and say strange things.
Finally, you get the word from the doctor that you are deceased.
Was this my time? Well, no. I eventually realized that a mistake
had been made, and got back to work.

Work meant returning to this project on the meaning of life,
and being told you're dead can make you think seriously about the
meaning of life! Many people who have gone through a clinical
death experience (flat-lining after a heart attack or other medical
crisis) say, after being revived, that they had been drawn to the
light of God's love. Their entire lives had flashed before their eyes.
They had realized that what truly matters is knowing and loving
God and others.

This sounds like the answer to the question which began this
book, "Why did God make you?" The answer: "God made me to
know, love, and serve him in this world..." We've been focusing on

love of God and ways to grow in our love of God. We've reflected on the importance of learning how much God loves us and on being in touch with the Trinity. We suggested the "Three-minute Trinity Prayer" as one way to do this. We mentioned the best possible way to grow in love of God, given by Jesus himself: Mass and Holy Communion. Next we discussed the practice of making spiritual communions. These ways can be important steps toward a real friendship with God here on earth, leading us to our ultimate destiny, to be happy with God forever in heaven.

FRIENDSHIP WITH GOD

Friends enjoy being with one another, and someone in love wants to be near the beloved always. That's not possible in human relationships, but it is possible with God. God is never out of reach, for "in him we live and move and have our being" (Acts 17:28). One of the reasons God gives us life here on earth is that we might grow into a deep friendship with him, one that will flow into eternity. We need to become more aware of God's presence and to be in touch with God. This may sound impossible for ordinary people. It is not.

It does mean we must develop our prayer life. Prayer is communication with God. The *Catechism of the Catholic Church* states that "the life of prayer is the habit of being in the presence of...God and in communion with him" (CCC 2565). This can be as easy and informal as the conversation of two good friends. Or it can involve the wonderful acts of sacramental worship given us by Jesus. As Catholics, we have vast resources for prayer at our disposal, and we should become more aware of them.

Even though prayer is an essential part of our friendship with God, I won't give a lengthy explanation of it here. Instead, I direct you to my book, *We Pray: Living in God's Presence*, also available from Liguori Publications. This book relies on the teachings of the Bible and *Catechism*, and uses stories, humor, and events from the everyday lives of real people to show how prayer can be an experience of God's presence that ultimately leads to the happiness of heaven.

The book includes a study of meditation, contemplation, centering prayer, the rosary, and other prayer methods from the Catholic tradition. We do need to set up a definite time for such prayer, a daily "appointment" with God. But that's not enough. God should be a part of everything we do, and we can be in constant conversation with God in our work, recreation, and even in our sleep. *We Pray* gives ideas for such conversation with God. Here I would like to offer an additional suggestion that can turn life's negatives into positives, and keep us in touch with God at the same time.

IF YOU KNOW HOW TO FRET OR WORRY...

There are some people who never fret or worry. I'm not one of them. It's easier for me to fret than to ignore life's foibles. It's easier for me to worry (especially about things over which I have no control) than to place the future in God's hands. So I try to follow the old advice, "Turn your worries into prayer."

In fact, fretting or worrying can actually lead us to God's presence and his desire to be in communion with us. The secret is to replace the negatives—the fretting and worrying—with prayer, especially short Bible verses where we allow God to speak to us and where we speak to God.

For example, if we are hurrying to an appointment, and there's a traffic accident ahead that brings everything to a stop, it's easy to fret and worry. But this won't make traffic move more quickly. It will only make our day more unpleasant. So why not replace the frustration with a Bible passage that reminds us of God's love such as this passage from Romans? "Who will separate us from the love of Christ? Will hardship, or distress, or persecution, or famine, or nakedness, or peril, or sword?...I am convinced that neither death, nor life...nor anything else in all creation, will be able to separate us from the love of God in Christ Jesus our Lord" (Romans 8:35,

38–39). This passage might quickly remind us that there are people facing far worse problems right now, like starvation, desperate poverty, and persecution. We could then talk to God about their plight, asking him to give them courage while giving us patience.

A second example might involve a relative or coworker who does something to offend us. Our first instinct might be anger and frustration, fretting about the harm done to us. Such negative emotions (as well as the desire to get even) do more harm to us than to the other person. It has been said that harboring ill feelings and resentment is like taking poison and waiting for the other person to die. The Christ-like response to injury is prayer, not revenge. We can replace any harsh feelings with Jesus' words, "Love one another as I have loved you" (John 15:12).

Memorizing Bible verses and repeating them is always a great way to pray, allowing God to speak to us and then responding to him. We have noted several passages that spotlight love, God's love for us and our love for God. If we reflect on and pray such passages, we'll be reminded of how God made us to know and love him. In the next chapter, I'll suggest more Bible passages that emphasize God's love.

And I'll keep trying to replace occasions for fretting and worrying with opportunities to reflect on God's love and to talk with Jesus. You might want to do the same.

I did have the appointment with my doctor. He came to the conclusion that I wasn't dead yet. But the mistake about my demise has been a blessing. It's reminded me that every day in this world is an opportunity to "know, love, and serve God," to grow in the love of God, and to look forward to the happiness that Jesus promises in heaven.

QUESTIONS FOR DISCUSSION AND REFLECTION

Have you ever had a near-death experience? Do you know anyone who has? What was the experience like? Who are some friends and relatives whose company you enjoy? Do you often recall that you live in God's presence? What are occasions and circumstances that cause you to fret or worry? Do you replace the fretting and worry with prayer?

ACTIVITIES

Think of something that has caused you to fret or worry in the past few days. Then replace it with this verse of Scripture: "Who will separate us from the love of Christ?" (Romans 8:35). Think of someone who has hurt you in some way. Pray this verse of Scripture as you become conscious of Christ's presence: "Love one another as I have loved you" (John 15:12).

CHAPTER II

God's Love by Night and by Day

A Catholic sister was doing missionary work in Bolivia. One night she had to stay in a storage shed that was crawling with rats. She reported that she didn't sleep a wink, but the rats didn't either, because she sat up all night saying, "Meow, meow."

Most of us probably don't have to deal with rats when we're trying to get a good night's sleep. But insomnia seems to be a common problem. Magazines advertise the latest medications to help people sleep, and remedies for sleeplessness are peddled on TV and radio.

However, difficulties in falling asleep at bedtime or after waking up in the middle of the night don't have to be all bad. I mentioned in Chapter 10 that those of us who fret and worry can learn to replace worries with prayer. So too, we can turn insomnia into an opportunity to enjoy God's love. Not a bad trade!

ONLY IN GOD WILL MY SOUL BE AT REST

Psalm 63 offers some wonderful verses that lead us into a loving nighttime dialogue with God. It begins with words of affection: "O God, you are my God, for you I long." The psalm then moves into recognition of God's great love for us: "For your love is better than life." Next come the verses that make this psalm a perfect prayer for nighttime: "On my bed I remember you. On you I muse through the night, for you have been my help. In the shadow of your wings I rejoice. My soul clings to you; your right hand upholds me" (Psalm 63:1, 3, 6–8; Grail translation).

Letting these verses drift through our consciousness can bring peace and rest. "Oh God, you are my God....Your love is better than life....On my bed I remember you. On you I muse through the night." These inspired words bring a quiet sense of well-being and can help anyone drift peacefully off to sleep, rejoicing in the shadow of God's wings, comforted by his love.

I read somewhere that there are three stages in life: 1) You have to take a nap and don't want to. 2) You want to take a nap but don't have the time. 3) You want to take a nap and have the time, but you can't fall asleep. If you are in stage three, try Psalm 63.

LOVING DIALOGUE WITH GOD

We can sleep in the care of God's love by reflecting on the inspired words of Scripture. We can then continue a loving dialogue with God during the day. Here are a few verses, easy to memorize, which emphasize God's love. Through them, God speaks to us.

- "I have loved you with an everlasting love" (Jeremiah 31:3).
- "...with everlasting love I will have compassion on you" (Isaiah 54:8).

After God says such words of love to us, we can reply, also from Scripture:

- "I love you, O Lord, my strength" (Psalm 18:1).
- "The earth, O Lord, is full of your steadfast love" (Psalm 119:64).

We can also reflect on passages that tell of God's love for us:

- "The steadfast love of the Lord never ceases" (Lamentations 3:22).
- "God proves his love for us in that while we still were sinners Christ died for us" (Romans 5:8).
- "God is love" (1 John 4:16).

A suitable prayer response to such passages might be:

- "I will sing of your steadfast love, O Lord, forever" (Psalm 89:1).

CHRIST'S LAST SUPPER DISCOURSE

God's most powerful affirmations of love were given by Jesus on the night before he died. The Last Supper Discourse, found in Chapters 14–17 of John's Gospel, is a beautiful love letter to you from Jesus. Try reading verse 9 of Chapter 15 in this way: "Dear (insert your name), as the Father has loved me, so I have loved you. Abide in my love." In Chapters 14–17, you can insert your name wherever you find pronouns like "them" or "you" that refer to the Apostles. Jesus will speak directly to you.

We must not miss the incredible power of these words. Jesus says he loves us as the Father loves him! In John 17:23, Jesus prays that the whole world may know the Father loves us as he loves Jesus. In John 14:16–17, Jesus promises to send us the Holy Spirit, the Comforter, who is God's Spirit of love. To leave no room for doubt, Jesus assures us: "No one has greater love than this, to lay down one's life for one's friends" (John 15:13).

If we could grasp the full meaning of these words, we'd be overwhelmed by God's love, as many saints have been. If we want to grow in God's love, we should think and pray about them. To do this, we can enter our "prayer room" (see Chapter 9), and invite Jesus to join us. Then we can listen as he speaks these words to us.

THE ROSARY: A PRAYER OF LOVE

The rosary is a beautiful prayer in itself. It is the Bible translated into prayer. But it has a dimension we may not have considered: the power to strengthen us in love of God. We might try seeing each mystery as an opportunity to reflect on God's love. For example, in the third Joyful Mystery, the birth of our Lord, we can think about how "...God so loved the world that he gave his only Son" (John 3:16). In the fifth Luminous Mystery, we see the Eucharist as Jesus' gift of himself, an amazing gift of love. In the fifth Sorrowful Mystery, we recall that no one has greater love than Jesus, who gave his life on the cross for us. In the third Glorious Mystery, we consider how Christ sends the Holy Spirit to dwell in our hearts, giving the life of God's love.

If we have allowed routine to slip into our recitation of the rosary, the conscious effort to meditate on God's love in every mystery can add new life to our prayer. It will help us to appreciate God's love for us and to expand our love for God.

FAMILY PRAYER

Any consideration of God's love should include family prayer, for God shares his love through family. These days, people are very busy and can forget that "the family that prays together stays together." At parish missions, I suggest that families and couples who are not praying together should begin now, but with a resolution they can keep, such as praying the Lord's Prayer together every day.

It can be enjoyable to pray together. After a recent parish mission, a couple informed me that they'd started praying the Our Father daily. They did it by alternating the phrases. Husband: "Our Father, who art in heaven." Wife: "Hallowed be thy name." And so on. If there are children, parents might alternate with children. But however we pray the Lord's Prayer, we should remember to consider the love God has for us, and how God wants us to love and forgive one another as he loves and forgives us.

After getting into the habit of saying the Lord's Prayer daily, ask Jesus to help you build on this foundation. Family prayer will deepen your love of God and one another.

ABIDING IN GOD'S LOVE, AWAKE OR ASLEEP

Frank and Linda told me that one night their three-year-old daughter Alex had trouble sleeping because she felt sick. They said she should ask God to help her get to sleep. She went back to her room and eventually fell asleep, only to wake up in the middle of the night. She went to her parents' room and wanted to get in bed with them. Asked what awakened her, she replied, "God helped me go to sleep, but then he woke me up." Whether awake or asleep, we abide in God's love.

God did indeed make us to know, love, and serve him. So far we've discussed knowing and loving God. In the next chapter, we'll begin a study of what it means to serve God.

QUESTIONS FOR DISCUSSION AND REFLECTION

When you have difficulty falling asleep or when you wake during the night, what do you do to get back to sleep? Have you tried praying, perhaps using memorized Scripture verses? Have you ever prayed passages from John 14–17 with special attention to the fact that Jesus speaks these words to you? Do you ever pray the rosary by meditating on how its mysteries reflect God's love for you? What is your opinion of the saying, "The family that prays together, stays together"?

ACTIVITIES

This chapter suggests a number of Scripture passages for use at nighttime. Such passages are effective ways at any time for God to speak to us, and for us to respond. Quietly turn to God and allow him to say to you, "I have loved you with an everlasting love" (Jeremiah 31:3). Then respond, "I love you, O Lord, my strength" (Psalm 18:1). Pray one mystery of the rosary, with special attention to how this mystery shows God's love for you. For a collection of meditations on each mystery of the rosary, see my book, *Christ's Mother and Ours* (Liguori Publications).

CHAPTER 12

God Made Me...
to Serve Him in This World

There are many reasons why people serve others. A teenage girl brought her new boyfriend home to meet her parents. They were appalled by his appearance: black leather jacket with skull and crossbones displayed on the back, tattoos everywhere, tongue studs and a nose ring. Later, the parents pulled their daughter aside and expressed their concern. "Dear," said the mother diplomatically, "he doesn't seem very nice." "Mom," replied the daughter, "if he wasn't nice, why would he be doing three thousand hours of community service?"

The boyfriend no doubt had a good reason for service! But the best reason is that God made us to know, love, and SERVE him. We have been reflecting on what it means to know and love God. Now we consider what it means to serve God. As we do, we must realize that knowledge and love of God are intimately connected to service of God and neighbor.

KNOWLEDGE AND SERVICE

"Now by this we may be sure that we know him, if we obey his commandments" (1 John 2:3). If we know the true God, we will keep the Ten Commandments; we will serve God. To the extent that we fail to keep the commandments, to that extent we really don't know God. Saint John bluntly asserts, "Whoever says, 'I have come to know him,' but does not obey his commandments, is a liar, and in such a person the truth does not exist" (1 John 2:4).

We have shown that there are many good reasons for belief in God, among them the findings of modern science. Here we should consider how the existence of God relates to service, and how objections to belief and service lack a solid foundation.

The philosophies of relativism and postmodernism are rampant today, especially in the media and higher education. These philosophies contend that there is no God, no absolute truth, no absolute right or wrong. People of today, especially the young, have been profoundly influenced by relativism and postmodernism. These philosophies undermine the foundations of our society, both civil and ecclesial, and also undercut our reasons to serve God.

Our country was founded on a declaration of truths that are real: "We hold these truths to be self-evident, that all men are created equal, that they are endowed by their Creator with certain unalienable Rights, that among these are Life, Liberty and the pursuit of Happiness." Our country could not long survive if, as relativism claims, truth and morality are not absolute, but a matter of personal opinion. Our Catholic Church relies on the words of Jesus, "I am the Truth" (John 14:6). Our faith is meaningless without the God who proclaims absolute truth and teaches what is right and wrong.

TRUTH OR OPINION

Unfortunately, many people deny the reality of absolute truth and morality. In an article in *Franciscan Way* Magazine (Spring 2008, pages 20–21), teacher Patrick Reis relates how he asked students in his government class at a Catholic high school: "Is there such a thing as absolute moral truth?" Almost all answered no. In this, they mirrored the finding of a 2002 national study of teenagers by Barna Research reporting that 83 percent of teens denied the existence of absolute moral truth and claimed that right or wrong depends on personal opinion.

Patrick's way of dealing with this was to assign an essay asking his students whether absolute moral truth exists. He graded their essays, and gave each student an "F." When they complained that he wasn't fair, he said he'd been convinced by their essays that what matters is personal opinion. His opinion was that they all deserved an "F."

They insisted this was unfair. He replied, "That's your opinion, and my opinion is as good as yours." He then announced that if they could come up with a solid argument against such relativism, he'd give the whole class an "A." After many false starts, a student finally pointed out that the relativist claim, "There is no absolute truth," is in itself an absolute statement. Much discussion followed, and the class agreed that there must be a basis for fairness apart from personal opinion. They agreed also that the source of such absolute truth must be beyond us; it must be the Creator mentioned in the Declaration of Independence. Jesus is (no surprise) right again. Knowing God is linked to keeping the commandments and to being fair.

LOVE AND SERVICE

The existence of absolute truth is essential to a life of service and meaning, and so is the reality of love and the ability to love. On the night before he died, Jesus said, "If you love me, you will keep my commandments" (John 14:15). If we love God, we will serve him by keeping the commandments. The more we love God, the easier it will be to serve God and keep the commandments. John tells us, "For the love of God is this, that we obey his commandments. And his commandments are not burdensome" (1 John 5:3).

Think of how parents serve the needs of children because the parents know and love them. Parents do things out of love that they might never do for pay. They feed and bathe and clothe a helpless infant. They are alert and watchful twenty-four hours a day, seven days a week. They get up, exhausted, in the middle of the night to attend to a wailing baby. They constantly place the needs of the child before their own.

Love is the free decision to reverence God and to put the well-being of others on a par with our own. Yet, some atheists and relativists deny the reality of love because they deny freedom. Human beings, they claim, are merely matter. Life, they say, was not created by God, but came about by chance. We may appear to make free choices, they contend, but we are deceived. Choices are not free, they continue, but are the result of biological and chemical forces and of the accidental clashing of atoms. Love is not real or possible. Parents don't truly love their children. They are simply machines that respond to physical stimuli.

Most people with common sense would dismiss this stance as ridiculous. But some members of the media and intelligentsia of today look down their noses at common sense and deny the foundations of love and of morality. This denial puts them (and anyone who follows them) into a sad coffin where life is deprived of value and joy, and where service becomes meaningless.

Their error is not new. The eighteenth century freethinker, Denis Diderot, lamented to his lady, "If I think that I love you of my own free will, I am mistaken. It is nothing of the sort.... It makes me wild to be entangled in a devil of a philosophy that my mind cannot deny and my heart gives lie to" (quoted in *The Purpose of It All*, by Stanley L. Jaki, p. 180). Anyone attracted to relativism and postmodernism ought to carefully consider where such philosophies inevitably lead. They lead to chaos and nihilism, to a tragic dead-end without truth, freedom, morality, or meaning. In contrast, Jesus gives us a key to the purpose of life, a reason to live, love, and serve, a plan and pattern for life. Jesus is the plan:"I am the light of the world. Whoever follows me will never walk in darkness but will have the light of life" (John 8:12). Jesus is the pattern: "I am the way, and the truth, and the life" (John 14:6).

Knowledge, Love, Service, and Prayer

We know that God made us to know, love, and serve him in this world, and to be happy with him forever in the next. This awareness is a treasure to be shared with others. Because we possess this treasure, we need to pray for people who are atheists and relativists that they might open their minds to know Jesus and their hearts to love him. Saint Paul offers us a prayer for this purpose:

> *For this reason I bow my knees before the Father....I pray that, according to the riches of his glory, he may grant that you may be strengthened in your inner being with power through his Spirit, and that Christ may dwell in your hearts through faith, as you are being rooted and grounded in love. I pray that you may have the power to comprehend, with all the saints, what is the breadth and length and height and depth, and to know the love of Christ that surpasses knowledge, so that you may be filled with all the fullness of God.*
>
> Ephesians 3:14, 16–19

We need also to pray for ourselves, turning to the Father, Son, and Holy Spirit for the knowledge and love that will inspire us to faithful service. Paul's prayer will serve well for this purpose if we change "you" to "we" and "your" to "our."

Bowing before the Father, strengthened by the Holy Spirit, one with Christ in faith and love, we will be ready for a lifetime of service to God and neighbor. And that includes community service!

QUESTIONS FOR DISCUSSION AND REFLECTION

How do you respond when someone says of issues like abortion and extra-marital sex: "One opinion is as good as another"? Is one opinion as good as another in moral matters? Why or why not? What do you think of teacher Patrick Reis's method of addressing relativism in his classroom? How do you explain objective truth and morality to people who say that objective truth and morality do not exist? What do you think Denis Diderot meant by his words quoted in this chapter? How might Jesus answer him?

ACTIVITIES

Consider the words from the Declaration of Independence quoted in this chapter. Ask yourself whether the Declaration of Independence would be passed in the Senate or House of Representatives today. Is "political correctness" right in ruling out mention of God?

You may wish to study postmodernism in more detail. It is a philosophy that encourages people to free themselves from every external authority, a world view that is based on the belief that there is no such thing as truth, no such thing as right or wrong. Believers in postmodernism claim that everything is relative, that there is no God, that chaos and confusion rule, and that there should be no one to answer to but one's own self. According to postmodernism, people create their own values, and when they are making choices, the only real consideration is "Does it feel good?" Compare this philosophy with the words of Jesus: "I am the way, and the truth, and the life" (John 14:6). Ask Jesus to help our society see God's truth and obey God's commandments. Pray for people who are relativists and atheists that they might open their minds and hearts to the truth and love of Jesus. You might use Paul's prayer in Ephesians 3:14–19 for this purpose.

CHAPTER 13

Service of God—Love of God

A toddler was throwing a tantrum at the supermarket checkout counter. Mom calmly said to the child as she led him to the exit, "You might as well give up on the crying. You're stuck with me for the next eighteen years."

Mom had patience and a sense of humor. Underlying that was clearly a deep love for her child. These qualities of hers offer a glimpse of God's care for us. In the Book of Exodus, we can almost hear God saying to the Israelites as he led them through the desert, "You might as well quit your crying and complaining. You're stuck with me forever."

The mother's love would never let her give up on her child. God's love will not let him give up on us. This is an important lesson to learn. Everything God does is done out of love. And that includes the commandments God gives to teach us how to serve him.

SERVING GOD, THE COMMANDMENTS, AND FREEDOM

A New Age "advisor" of youth has proclaimed that there is no right or wrong and no such thing as disobeying God. "Why would God give you freedom, and then take away your freedom by giving you commandments?" This foolish misguidance portrays the Ten Commandments as restrictive and unloving. The truth is that keeping the commandments and serving God brings true freedom. When people do not serve God, they imprison themselves behind bars of sin and selfishness.

What is the proper approach to serving God, to obeying God's commandments? The answer can be found in the Exodus stories that precede God's giving of the Ten Commandments. The Israelites had been slaves in Egypt. God liberated them, then gave them the commandments to keep them from falling into a worse slavery, that of sin. The commandments did not take away freedom, but gave it.

It may be helpful to make a distinction between "freedom from" and "freedom for." The first is built on the notion that freedom means the ability to do anything without restraint. The second means that God has given us freedom to make good choices. The first is the "freedom" espoused by Satan: "I will not serve." The second is the freedom taught by Jesus: "If you continue in my word, you are truly my disciples; and you will know the truth, and the truth will make you free" (John 8:31–32).

As for advice to youth, I ask them to imagine this situation: It is your graduation day, and your parents give you a brand new convertible. Would you want to drive that beautiful new car across the country on a day when there are absolutely no traffic laws to restrict you? You can go as fast as you want. So can everybody else. Truckers can drive their eighteen wheelers eastbound in the westbound lane at one hundred miles per hour. Anyone can make a left turn or a U-turn at will. No laws. Complete freedom!

But I've never found a teen who would want to drive that new car under those conditions. Why? Because when there are no laws, there is no freedom. You can go nowhere. Good traffic laws don't destroy freedom. They give people the freedom to travel. And so it is on the road of life. God's commandments don't take away freedom. They make us free.

THE COMMANDMENTS AND LOVE

Commandments that bring freedom flow from God's love for us. In the case of the supermarket toddler, his mother's love directed him away from tantrums which, if unchecked, would eventually control his life. God's love directs us from the bondage of sin and guides us to the freedom of God's children. Obedience to God, serving God, keeps us truly free for the happiness God wants for us here and forever.

When we realize that serving God means responding to One who loves us as dear children and who wants freedom and happiness for us more than we do, serving God takes on a whole new meaning. The Bible presents many images to help us appreciate God's love. God is our Father (Hosea 11:1; Matthew 6:9). Jesus is our brother, because his Father is our Father. The Holy Spirit dwells in us (John 14:17).

The Bible also uses the imagery of marriage to describe God's relationship with us. In the Old Testament, God is presented as a husband who never gives up on his spouse, the people of Israel (Hosea 2:16–20). In the New Testament, the Church is the spouse of Christ (Luke 5:34) and the "bride of the Lamb" (Revelation 21:9).

Serving God is not slavery to a harsh master. It is not a burden. It is rather the choice to live in a way that will bring true freedom, real happiness, and life with purpose and meaning. Serving God is not obeying laws because we fear punishment. It is rather the compliance of a loving child to the wishes of doting parents. It is the ready willingness of loving spouses to do whatever they can for each other.

I've seen this kind of ready willingness in newlyweds, and also in the loving concern of elderly people who go daily to the local nursing home to help care for an infirm spouse. When I have complimented them, they express surprise that I would suppose their service to be a burden. It is a work of love for them.

I've been blessed to know Catholics who feel the same way about living their faith. For them, going to Mass, helping out at church activities, teaching religion, serving the needy, keeping the commandments, and other ways of serving God are not burdens, but sources of joy. When I see such believers, I realize that I have a long way to go in my own attempts to serve God. There are times when I feel sorry for myself because my efforts seem to be unsuccessful or unappreciated. Deep down I know that if I loved and served God better, I'd be more ready to do my best and leave the results up to God. I'd also be a lot happier.

LEARNING THE HABIT OF JOYFUL SERVICE

How can we enjoy a life of loving service to God? One important way is to be more responsive to God's invitation to the intimacy felt by loving spouses or by children and caring parents. When we are aware of God's love, when we remember that God is always near, we'll find it much easier to serve God and to find joy in such service.

The saints called this the practice of the presence of God. This practice is closely connected to prayer. The *Catechism* says that "the life of prayer is the habit of being in the presence of...God" (CCC 2565). The practice of the presence of God is also important for a life of service. A mother finds it easy to serve the needs of an infant she holds in her arms. A young man readily attends to the wishes of his future bride while they are together on a date. We will more readily serve God when we are constantly aware of God's nearness.

Some people remind themselves of God's presence when they hear the sound of bells or the chiming of a clock. Others think of God when they drive past a church. A crucifix on the wall, a statue on the dashboard, a computer screen-saver can bring God's presence to mind. Each time I unlock a door, I try to recall the words of Pope John Paul II: "Open the doors to Christ." In these and in many other ways, we can keep in our consciousness the love of God.

The goal is to associate service with love. We are on the way to that goal when hearing the phrase, "keeping the commandments," brings a smile because it makes us think of God as a loving Father. We are on the way when the command to forgive our enemies calls to mind the loving sacrifice of Jesus on the cross. We are on the way when a challenge brings, not weariness or fear, but the energy of the Holy Spirit: "The Spirit God gives is no cowardly spirit, but One that makes us strong, loving, and wise" (see 2 Timothy 1:7).

"GOD MADE ME...TO SERVE HIM... AND TO BE HAPPY FOREVER"

In future chapters, we'll examine the Church's teaching on how to serve God. The *Catechism* calls this "Life in Christ." As we move ahead, let's hear God saying, with a voice full of humor and love: "Enjoy serving me. You might as well. You're stuck with me forever!"

QUESTIONS FOR DISCUSSION AND REFLECTION

How would you respond to someone who says that God's commandments are meaningless because God would not give freedom and then limit it with commands to do this or not do that? The chapter uses traffic laws as a way of explaining to teens that laws give freedom. Can you think of other ways to do this? In your own words, can you explain how faith and the commandments are linked? Can you explain how love and the commandments are linked? Do you know friends or relatives who serve God joyfully, seeing such service as a privilege rather than a burden? What are your favorite ways (like the chiming of a clock) of being reminded of God's presence?

ACTIVITIES

Place yourself in God's presence. Then ask the Father to show you how the commandments are signs of his love and the path to true freedom. Look at a crucifix and ask Jesus to touch you with his love, helping you to follow him. Remember the Holy Spirit dwelling within you and ask for the courage and energy to face any challenge.

CHAPTER 14

Service of God—Life in Christ

B enedict XVI was elected Pope on April 19, 2005, about six months after the St. Louis Cardinals were swept by the Boston Red Sox in the 2004 World Series. I was preaching a parish mission at St. Mary's Church in Cape Girardeau, Missouri, during the papal election. At the end of the week, a teacher told me she was asked by a first grader, "Why did the Cardinals get to elect the Pope when the Red Sox won the World Series?"

The St. Louis Cardinals lost the World Series, but the cardinals in Rome, guided by the Holy Spirit, picked a winner! For Pope Benedict XVI, election to the papacy meant a new opportunity to proclaim Jesus Christ as Savior. When he visited the United States in April, 2008, Benedict spoke to young people in Yonkers, New York. He emphasized something we've been considering in this book, that serving Jesus Christ brings truth, freedom, life, and love. He said:

Dear friends, truth is not an imposition. Nor is it simply a set of rules. It is the discovery of the One who never fails us, the One whom we can always trust. In seeking truth we come to live by belief because ultimately truth is a person: Jesus Christ. That is why authentic freedom is not an opting out. It is an opting in; nothing less than letting go of self and allowing oneself to be drawn into Christ's very being for others....Sometimes we are looked upon as people who speak only of prohibitions. Nothing could be further from the truth! Authentic Christian discipleship is marked by a sense of wonder. We stand before the God we know and love as a friend, the vastness of his creation and the beauty of our Christian faith.

WWW.VATICAN.VA

Jesus Christ IS truth. Choosing to follow him gives freedom, for it liberates us from the prison of self-centeredness. Choosing to follow Jesus means "opting in," allowing oneself to be drawn into Christ's life. This is a life of love, of service to God and others. It leads ultimately to heaven, to eternal union with the Father, Son, and Holy Spirit.

This is another way of saying that God made us to know, love, and serve him in this world and to be happy with him forever. Here as in all things Catholic, we look to Jesus. That's why the third section of the *Catechism* about how to serve God is called "Life in Christ."

LIFE IN CHRIST

The English translation of the *Catechism of the Catholic Church* was published in 1994. The *Catechism* is a marvelous resource for anyone wanting to learn Church teaching. It is divided into four main parts as discussed in this book's Introduction. The first, "The Profession of Faith," explains the beliefs of the Church as found in the Creed. We are created as God's children, given new life by Christ, and made holy by the Spirit. The second part, "The Celebration of the Christian Mystery," shows how the sacraments of the Church communicate the Father's love, the grace of Christ, and the gifts of the Spirit. The third part, "Life in Christ," teaches us how to live as Christ teaches, as members of his body, the Church. Finally, the fourth part, "Christian Prayer," shows us how to pray in union with Christ.

Here we focus on part three, "Life in Christ." In this and in succeeding chapters we will spotlight important points in the third part of the *Catechism* and summarize the Church's teaching found there. Hopefully, this will encourage you to study the *Catechism* in depth. After all, we are exploring one of life's most important questions: How should we live?

The answer, the *Catechism* affirms, is a matter of life and death (CCC 1696). In this, the *Catechism* follows Moses, who said to the Israelites just before they entered the Promised Land: "I call heaven and earth to witness that I set before you life and death....Choose life then, that you and your descendants may live" (Deuteronomy 30:19). We choose life and learn Christ's way by studying what he teaches through his Church.

WE ARE MADE IN GOD'S IMAGE...TO BE HAPPY

In previous chapters, we've seen how atheists deny not only the existence of God but the reality of truth and freedom. The Church teaches that we are not accidents resulting from nothingness and mindless evolution. Rather, we are created in God's image and likeness, especially because God has given us an intellect to know the truth and a free will to choose what is right and good.

Knowledge and the freedom to choose are related to our desire for happiness. We all want to be happy. That's because God made us "to be happy forever with him in heaven." The *Catechism* spotlights the Beatitudes (Matthew 5:3–12) as pathways to the happiness made possible by God's grace. The Beatitudes shape us to become more like Jesus and give us the promised joy of seeing God forever in heaven. Since we have been made to know, love, and serve God, real happiness can be found in doing God's will, not in riches, fame, or power.

The Beatitudes can be hard to understand, and we must view them as Jesus lived them. For example, the first Beatitude, "Blessed are the poor in spirit, for theirs is the kingdom of heaven," refers to those who recognize their dependence on God. On the cross, Jesus completely submitted himself to God: "Father, into your hands I commend my spirit" (Luke 23:46). Thus, Jesus shows that in every circumstance we find peace and joy when we recognize our dependence on God and place our lives in his hands. (For an explanation of the Beatitudes and how good people live them today, see my book, *The Search For Happiness*, pages 120–126).

HUMAN FREEDOM

The *Catechism* defines freedom as the power, rooted in intellect and will, to perform deliberate actions for which we are responsible. Freedom allows us to choose between good and evil. Doing good makes us truly free, while doing evil makes us slaves of sin. The ability to make free choices distinguishes us as humans from lower animals.

Because freedom is God's gift, we are responsible to God for our acts to the extent that they are voluntary. Freedom and responsibility can be diminished or nullified by ignorance, force, fear, habit, and other factors like economic, social, political, and cultural conditions. Every human being has the right to exercise freedom, and this right, especially in moral and religious matters, must be respected. But freedom does not mean the license to do or say anything, right or wrong. Christ has redeemed us from the bonds of sin and given us real freedom. His grace enables us to use our freedom properly, choosing what is true and good.

THE MORALITY OF HUMAN ACTS

Human acts are morally good or evil depending on their object, intention, and circumstances. The object is what a person chooses: a good act such as almsgiving or an evil one such as theft. The intention is the act of the will, one's purpose in choosing an object. A bad intention can cause a good act to become sinful, as when a person gives alms merely to win praise. On the other hand, a good intention cannot justify something which is evil in itself. For example, the desire to ease suffering does not justify the murder of the elderly. Circumstances are secondary elements of a moral act and contribute to the goodness or evil of that act. The amount taken in a theft, for example, helps determine the degree of sinfulness. Force or fear can diminish one's guilt. Object, intention, and circumstances determine the morality of human acts, and all three must be good for an action to be good.

TO LIVE IS CHRIST

The St. Louis Cardinals may have lost the World Series in 2004, but we never lose when we follow Christ. To serve God is to experience "Life in Christ." The *Catechism of the Catholic Church* will be our guide as we see how knowledge and love of God lead to joyful service and happiness with God forever.

QUESTIONS FOR DISCUSSION AND REFLECTION

What do you think Pope Benedict meant when he said that authentic freedom is not an opting out, but an opting in? Can you list the subject matter contained in each of the four main parts of the *Catechism of the Catholic Church*? Can you give examples of how freedom and responsibility for actions might be diminished by ignorance, by force, or by fear? How can a good object, like almsgiving, become sinful because of one's intention or by circumstances?

ACTIVITIES

Many of the ideas in this chapter were based on the *Catechism*, numbers 1691–1761. You may look through this part of the *Catechism* for an in-depth presentation of these ideas. In prayer, ask the Holy Spirit to guide you as you study life in Christ, helping you to make the object, intention, and circumstances of this study as grace-filled as possible.

CHAPTER 15

Service of God and Moral Living

A class of second-graders was asked by their religion teacher, "What is conscience?" A girl raised her hand and said, "Conscience is the voice that tells you to stop when you are beating up your little brother. My conscience has saved him many times." A boy added, "Conscience is something that makes you tell your mother what you did before your sister tells her."

Even small children know the difference between right and wrong. But as we grow older, living a moral life gets more complicated. We are blessed as Catholics to have time-tested principles about conscience and moral living. These are outlined in the *Catechism*. We begin to examine them now.

CONSCIENCE

Conscience is sometimes portrayed as a little angel, whispering what we should do and avoid. Actually, conscience is a judgment of our reason whereby we recognize whether an action is good or evil. If we seek divine truth, God will guide us in our conscience toward good and away from evil. Conscience includes knowing the principles of morality, applying them in given circumstances, and making judgments about whether an action is good or evil. Conscience enables us to take responsibility for our deeds. If we do evil, conscience calls us to repentance.

Faced with moral choices, it is possible for a person's conscience to make a right or wrong judgment. Making a proper judgment can be difficult, but we must always seek what is right according to God's will. In this we are helped by the virtue of prudence, the advice of wise counselors, the guidance of the Holy Spirit, and clear norms such as the Golden Rule. We have an obligation to form our conscience properly through Scripture and the Church's teaching.

If we are responsible for any ignorance that causes us to make wrong judgments of conscience, we are also responsible to God for the evil actions that result. If we are not to blame for our ignorance, we are not guilty of sin. We are obliged by God to know our Faith to the best of our ability, be aware of Catholic moral principles, and be guided by Christ-like standards of moral conduct.

VIRTUES

Virtues are good habits that help us to do the right thing. The *Catechism* offers two main categories of virtues, human and theological. Human virtues are those which guide our conduct according to reason and faith. They help us to lead a good life more easily and joyfully.

Four human virtues are so significant that they are called the cardinal virtues (from the Latin word for "hinge," because so many other virtues hinge on them):

- Prudence helps us discern the right thing to do in any circumstance and guides our conscience in making judgments.
- Justice enables us to give God and others their due.
- Fortitude strengthens us to do good, to weather life's difficulties and temptations, and to overcome fear.
- Temperance helps us to control our desires and to use the good things of life in a Christ-like way.

The three theological virtues are so named because they are gifts of God and direct our relationship to God:

- By faith we believe in God and accept the truths that God reveals.

We express our faith by professing it, by good works, and by sharing it with others.

- By hope we desire heaven as our final goal and have confident assurance of achieving it with God's help. Hope keeps us from falling into despair on the one hand, or from presumption on the other.
- By charity we love God above all and our neighbor as ourselves. True charity is modeled on Christ's unconditional love and helps us keep God's law faithfully.

While the theological virtues are gifts of God, we can open ourselves to these gifts by prayer, by reception of the sacraments, and by imitating Mary and the saints through lives built on faith, hope, and charity.

Spiritual guides speak of the "practice of virtue." Virtues are habits, and we are able to practice them by learning the essential qualities of each and by performing virtuous acts until they become second nature. Just as someone becomes adept at a sport by learning the basics and practicing them, so we grow in the virtues by learning and practicing them. The better we learn the basic tenets of our faith, from the Bible and the *Catechism*, and the more we practice virtue, the easier it becomes to live the virtues. And just as an athlete can improve his or her proficiency by watching skilled professionals in action, so we can become more proficient in the practice of virtue by studying the life of Jesus and the lives of the saints.

Athletes perform better when they are nourished by a proper diet. We practice virtue more easily when we are strengthened and sustained by God's grace. We receive this spiritual "food of grace" through prayer and the sacraments and above all through the frequent reception of the living Bread from heaven, the Body of Christ.

Our efforts to practice virtue are sustained by the gifts of the Holy Spirit. These are mentioned in Scripture and explained in the *Catechism*. The gifts are wisdom, understanding, counsel, fortitude, knowledge, piety, and fear of the Lord (see Isaiah 11:2 and CCC

1831). They are called gifts because they are granted as permanent dispositions in baptism and confirmation by the Holy Spirit. But we must practice them as virtues, or they will remain dormant. Activated by attentiveness to the Spirit and by prayer, they help us to think, speak, and act like Jesus.

The Spirit's love within us produces traits called the fruits of the Holy Spirit. They are charity, joy, peace, patience, kindness, goodness, generosity, gentleness, faithfulness, modesty, self-control, and chastity (see Galatians 5:22–23 and CCC 1832). They are virtues, of course, but as "fruits" they are viewed as qualities that grow primarily from a loving relationship with the Holy Spirit and secondarily from our own efforts.

SIN

When we sin, we disobey God's law, reject God's love, and prefer ourselves over God and neighbor. Sin is the worst of evils and must never be underestimated. Its wickedness was most evident when it caused Christ's passion and death. Every sin is rooted in the rejection of God's love, the misuse of freedom, and the choice of evil over good.

Sins are evaluated in terms of their gravity. Mortal sins are those which are so serious that they destroy love within us and turn us away from God, who is our final goal. For a sin to be mortal, three conditions must be present. First, it must constitute a grave matter, something that causes significant harm to others or ourselves or is a serious affront to God (for example, murder, adultery, blasphemy). Second, there must be full knowledge; the sinner must be aware of the wickedness of the action. Third, there must be complete consent of the will; the sinner must freely choose to do what is evil. Mental deficiency, unintentional ignorance, passion, and external forces can diminish the gravity of sin. But when grave matter, full knowledge, and complete consent are present, mortal sin exists and can cause eternal death for those who do not repent. Refusal to repent is that sin against the Holy Spirit for which Jesus says there is no forgiveness. Impenitence by its nature rejects God's mercy and embraces eternal death.

Venial sins are failings which do not destroy love or sever our bond of love with God. They involve less serious matter (such as theft of a small item), lack of full knowledge, or incomplete consent. Venial sins can weaken our friendship with God and lead to more serious failings, so we should try to overcome them with the help of God's grace.

Some people question the distinction between mortal and venial sins. But the Bible makes distinctions about the severity of various sins. Saint John writes: "All wrongdoing is sin, but there is a sin that is not mortal" (1 John 5:17). Saint Paul lists a number of grave sins in Galatians 5:19–21, then states that "those who do such things will not inherit the kingdom of God." The distinction is also based on common sense: It is certainly less serious for a child to steal a piece of candy than for a murderer to kill an innocent person.

Each act of sin inclines us to sin again. Habits of sin are called vices, which stand in contrast to the virtues they undermine. Vices are often associated with the capital sins of pride, avarice, envy, wrath, lust, gluttony, and sloth. Though sin is personal, it often involves cooperation with others and produces evil social structures that cause sin to multiply.

PASSIONS

In traditional theology, passions refer to emotions or feelings that incline us either to act or to refrain from acting. Among these are love and hatred, desire and fear, sadness and anger. They can spring up suddenly and unbidden, and as such are neither good nor evil in themselves. They become good or evil when we are aware of them and guide them by reason and will. Passions become morally good when they contribute to a virtuous act and evil when they contribute to a sinful act. Jesus' anger was good because it helped motivate him to drive dishonest merchants from the Temple. Cain's anger was evil because it impelled him to murder his brother, Abel. Strong feelings are not necessary for morality or holiness, but in the Christian life, our passions, mobilized by the Holy Spirit, can attract us to God and to moral goodness.

MORALITY AND THE HUMAN COMMUNITY

The second graders who started this chapter linked conscience to relationships, to community. The moral life is based on God's love, and God's love forms the perfect Community, the Trinity. So morality, as we shall see, leads us to a consideration of community.

QUESTIONS FOR DISCUSSION AND REFLECTION

What does the statement, "Conscience is a judgment of our reason," mean to you? How many differences can you find between human virtues and theological virtues? In what ways are virtues, gifts of the Holy Spirit, and fruits of the Holy Spirit similar? In what ways are they different? Can you explain in your own words the meaning of sin, as well as the distinction between mortal and venial sin? Is this chapter's understanding of the passions the same as the society's common understanding of the same word?

ACTIVITIES

The issues explained in this chapter are treated in the *Catechism*, numbers 1762–1876. You may wish to study these paragraphs in detail. Consider the following terms and try to give a brief explanation of each in your own words: conscience, virtues, sin, passions. If necessary, review the definitions given in Chapter 15. The chapter states that we are obliged by God to know the truth and live by it. Bible passages to this effect are countless. See, for example, Deuteronomy 6:4–7 and 1 Timothy 4:6–11.

CHAPTER 16

God's Love, Social Justice, and the Law

There is a story that during the Second World War, British, American, French and Russian soldiers would sometimes share jeeps for military police duty. The soldiers, except the Russian, would tell jokes to pass the time. The American asked, "What's the matter with you, Ivan? Doesn't anything funny happen in Russia? Don't you have any jokes?" "Have you ever heard of the great canals in Russia?" asked Ivan. "Yes," answered the American. "It must have been a hard job building them." "Exactly," said Ivan. "They were built by people who told jokes."

There are many jokes about communism, but communism is no joke. It has brought untold misery to nations and caused tens of millions of deaths through wars, labor camps, and genocide. It is an unjust system, a powerful example of why morality is not just a personal matter, but one of community, calling for social justice.

THE CATECHISM AND HUMAN COMMUNITY

The *Catechism of the Catholic Church* explains that we are made in God's image and likeness. Just as God is a community of Persons, so we are created as persons who need community and society. A society is a group of persons bound together by a principle of unity that goes beyond each individual. Through society, people help one another, receive benefits from ancestors, and pass them on to future generations.

Some societies, like the family and the state, flow from human nature and are necessary for survival. Other societies relating to economic, social, cultural, recreational, and political goals arise from the natural tendency to form beneficial associations. All social institutions should exist for the sake of individual persons. Here is where communism fails so badly, as it makes the individual exist for the sake of the state.

Communism also violates the principle of subsidiarity, which is important in Catholic social teaching. This principle states that what can be done by a smaller body should not be taken over by a larger one, and that larger societal groups should support smaller ones in striving for the common good.

Society needs legitimate authority to maintain order, promote the common good, enact just laws, and enforce them. The fact that authority comes from God demands obedience and respect for those in authority. It also demands that leaders, on their part, should work for the benefit of societal members, not for selfish purposes. Because God shares power with humanity, leaders must share their authority, and they should be chosen by citizens.

All societies must respect spiritual values, which are more crucial to our survival and happiness than are secular values. Different forms of government are acceptable as long as they serve the good of their communities and do nothing contrary to God's law. In any political structure, there should be a balance of power that keeps authority within proper limits.

For authority to be legitimate, it must seek the common good, which is the sum total of social conditions that allow people as individuals and groups to achieve fulfillment. It consists of three elements: respect for the rights of the human person, development of the spiritual and material well-being of society, and establishment of peace, justice, and security.

Increasing human interdependence calls for a community of nations that can advance the common good of humanity, always placing the good of individuals before that of the state. At every level of society, personal involvement is needed. People must take charge of areas where they have responsibility, such as their families and occupations. They should also participate in public life, working to eliminate evils like abortion and promote godly values.

SOCIAL JUSTICE

Social justice is respect for the human person and for the God-given rights which flow from human dignity. Social justice refers especially to the rights of people in their relationship to society and to various associations. Society must provide the conditions for social justice, so that individuals and associations obtain what is rightfully theirs.

Respect for others comes from the principle that each person must consider the neighbor as another self. Further, Jesus teaches us to offer special concern for the disadvantaged and to show love to all, even enemies. Any system—whether atheistic communism or unbridled capitalism—that ignores such Christian values, is unacceptable.

Because human beings have the same nature, origin, destiny, and dignity, every form of discrimination ought to be eliminated. But people have different talents and abilities. They must work together generously to help one another, to eradicate sinful inequalities, and to promote human solidarity.

Solidarity introduces concepts like friendship and social charity to our understanding of social justice. It includes the just distribution of goods, fair pay for services, and peaceful striving for a just social order at every level of society. It entails the sharing of spiritual goods even more than material goods. The Church offers the good news and rich blessings of our faith to all for their spiritual and temporal welfare.

THE MORAL LAW

A quick look through any daily newspaper will show that our world is far from what it should be. We want peace, but terrorism and war abound. We long for security, but crime makes us fearful and uneasy. We seek happiness, but find it hard to achieve.

We have been created for peace, security, and happiness, but these are out of the reach of merely human efforts. We need God's help. We need salvation. God offers grace to sustain us and law to guide us. Law may be defined as a rule of conduct passed by competent authority for the sake of the common good. Moral law prescribes actions which lead to eternal happiness. It prohibits evil deeds which separate us from God. It finds expression in God's eternal law, in natural law, in revealed law, and in civil and ecclesiastical laws.

Natural law is the law written on the soul of every person. It enables us to discern good from evil, right from wrong, and to grasp the basic precepts governing a moral life. It is the light of understanding placed in us by God, showing us what we should do and what we should avoid. Its fundamental principles are common to all cultures and every age. It provides the foundation for upright living, human community, and civil law. But because its precepts are not easily perceived by everyone, God has revealed some additional laws to direct us with clarity and certainty.

GOD'S REVEALED LAW: THE OLD AND NEW TESTAMENTS

God revealed law to guide us on the way to eternal happiness. We find the first stage of this law in the Old Testament. It is summed up in the Ten Commandments and expresses many truths naturally accessible to reason. The Old Law is imperfect, pointing out obligations without offering the grace to fulfill them, but it prepared humanity for the Gospel.

The Law of the Gospel, the New Law, is the perfection of the divine law, and calls us to imitate the perfection of our heavenly Father. We find it expressed most clearly in Christ's Sermon on the Mount (Matthew 5–7). It is further elaborated in New Testament passages such as Romans 12–15, 1 Corinthians 12–13, Colossians 3–4, and Ephesians 4–5. It is summed up in the Golden Rule, "Do unto others as you would have them do unto you." It calls us to new heights of holiness through Jesus' command to love others as he loves us.

LOVE AND THE LAW

The New Law is a law of love because it originates in the loving heart of God the Father. It is expressed in the life and teachings of Jesus Christ, the Son of God who loves all people even to death on the cross. Its observance is made possible by the loving grace of the Holy Spirit, who dwells in the souls of believers.

God is love. Catholic principles of social justice and of law are linked to the love of God. "The commandment we have from him is this: those who love God must love their brothers and sisters also" (1 John 4:21). And that's no joke. It is God's gift!

QUESTIONS FOR DISCUSSION AND REFLECTION

What principles of social justice discussed in this chapter make communism unacceptable? How can unbridled capitalism violate the principles of social justice? What are some ways in which a government might violate the principle of subsidiarity? What makes authority legitimate? What are some failings which can make an authority illegitimate, at least in certain areas of life and social relationships? Is there a religious basis to the statement that people have a right to choose their political leaders?

ACTIVITIES

You may study the concepts outlined in this chapter in numbers 1877–1986 of the *Catechism*. Try to give a definition of these terms: society, common good, social justice, human solidarity, law, moral law, natural law, revealed law, Old Law, and New Law.

CHAPTER 17

Serving God...
With God's Help

Jennifer Fulwider was an abortion advocate and an atheist. She became a Christian and then realized how she had deceived herself into claiming that abortion was not murder. She "became stunned to the point of feeling physically ill upon witnessing the level of evil that normal people can support...educated professionals calmly justifying infanticide by calling the victims fetuses instead of babies" (www.americamagazine.org/content/article.cfm?article_id=10904).

Recognizing such self-deception should cause us to look inward. We have been damaged by the original sin of our first parents. We too can deceive ourselves. We may not condone abortion, but we can find ways of justifying our own sins of gossip, dishonesty, sloth, and worse.

Consider the old ditty:

I dreamed death came the other night,
and heaven's gate swung open wide.
An angel winged, with halo bright,
did usher me inside.
And there to my astonishment
stood folks I'd judged and labeled
as quite unfit, of little worth,
and spiritually disabled.
Indignant words rose to my lips,

but never were set free.
For every face showed stunned surprise.
No one expected me.

Yes, we can have false notions of our own superiority. We too can be deceived. We, along with the rest of humanity, are capable of manipulating notions of natural law and God's law to suit ourselves. We need God's wisdom and guidance to find the truth and hold fast to it. That's why Jesus, the Way, Truth, and Life, established his Church to teach and guide us.

THE CHURCH: TEACHER AND GUIDE

Jesus built the Church on Peter and his successors, promising that hell would not prevail against it (Matthew 16:18). He told the Apostles, "Whoever listens to you listens to me" (Luke 10:16). Jesus gave us the Church as "the pillar and bulwark of the truth" (1 Timothy 3:15).

The Church teaches God's law in ways clear and unmistakable. The Magisterium, the official teaching office of the Church, explains the basic tenets of natural law, applies the Ten Commandments to modern challenges, and presents Catholic moral principles consistent with the teaching of Jesus. The Church helps us to know God and understand God's will so we may serve him properly. But knowledge is not enough. We are trapped in a flood of sinfulness. Saint Paul observes, "For I do not do the good I want, but the evil I do not want is what I do....Wretched man that I am! Who will rescue me from this body of death?" (Romans 7:19, 24).

THE CHURCH: MINISTER OF GOD'S LOVE AND GRACE

The story of Adam and Eve's original sin shows that the first human beings knew God's will, but refused to do it. Through their disobedience, sin entered the world, followed by all the evils resulting from sin. To us as individuals, sin brings unhappiness. To society, sin brings alienation, crime, and war. Instead of living as God's children, we are cut off from God. Instead of being a family, we are enemies to one another. Caught in the flood of that original sin, we cannot save ourselves. That's why Paul speaks of "this body of death." We need salvation.

God offers salvation through his Son. Jesus does not just tell us what to do, but gives the means to do God's will. Jesus brings forgiveness of sins, new life for us as God's children, and the grace that enables us to love and serve God and one another.

God's grace cleansing us from original sin and communicating righteousness through baptism is called justification. In baptism, we are justified (made just and holy in God's sight) by being united to Christ's Passion, thereby dying to sin. We are united to his resurrection by rising to new life as members of his body. As the *Catechism* teaches (CCC 1987–1995), justification frees us from sin and confers God's righteousness, empowering us to live in God's love.

With justification come faith, hope, charity, and obedience to God's will and collaboration between God's grace and our freedom. We can do nothing without God's grace, but once justified, we can freely cooperate with that grace. Justification leads to our salvation as we follow the guidance of the Holy Spirit, given to us by Christ in baptism.

GRACE, MERIT, AND HOLINESS

By the grace of justification we leave sin behind and begin to live in God's sanctifying grace. This is God's free and undeserved favor making us adoptive children of God, sharers of the divine nature, and heirs of heaven. It is called sanctifying grace because it makes us holy as we participate in the life of the Trinity. Because it is a stable disposition that perfects the soul and enables it to live in union with God, it is also called habitual grace.

Sanctifying grace is distinguished from actual graces, God's special helps that assist us as we follow Christ. Actual graces inspire people to turn away from sin and to accept God's life and love. They sustain us in God's sanctifying grace. Among the actual graces are sacramental graces, which are conferred by the seven sacraments in ways specific to each sacrament. There are special graces called charisms, gifts granted for the common good of the Church. There are graces of state, which enable us to fulfill responsibilities of Christian life and of church ministries such as teaching and service.

God has chosen to involve us in his plan of salvation and to reward us for our good deeds. In this sense, we merit blessings and benefits from God. Merit refers to the reward owed someone for a good act. Strictly speaking, God owes us nothing, because all we have comes from God. But God allows us to merit graces and blessings. God rewards us for cooperating with his grace because he loves us.

Because we are God's beloved children, he gives us the right to eternal life as a result of our cooperation. Assisted by the Holy Spirit we can merit for ourselves and others the graces needed for sanctification and eternal life. All this comes from Jesus and through him. We cannot merit the initial grace of justification, which is pure gift, and if Jesus had not made it possible for us to become children of God, we could merit nothing at all.

Life is a call to holiness, to be perfect as our heavenly Father is perfect (Matthew 5:48). Growth in holiness leads to intimate union with Christ. It always includes the cross and requires penance and prayer. We strive for holiness. We strive to know, love, and serve God, trusting that God will give us the grace of final perseverance and the joy of eternal life.

JUSTIFICATION AND SALVATION

Catholics believe justification is the first step toward salvation (eternal happiness in heaven). Some Christians, however, identify salvation with "accepting Jesus as Lord and Savior." In Romans 10:9, Paul states that "...if you confess with your lips that Jesus is Lord and believe in your heart that God raised him from the dead, you will be saved." In Romans 10:13 he writes: "Everyone who calls on the name of the Lord shall be saved." But what does it mean to confess and believe and call on? It means more than merely saying words. The words must lead to works. How do we love? By expressing love in our actions. How do we believe? By expressing faith in our actions. That's why Paul writes to the Philippians: "Work out your own salvation with fear and trembling" (Philippians 2:12).

We are not saved by faith or works. We are saved by the grace of Jesus Christ. We access that grace by faith, and our faith is real only when it finds expression in good works.

Jesus warned: "Not everyone who says to me, `Lord, Lord,' will enter the kingdom of heaven, but only the one who does the will of my Father in heaven" (Matthew 7:21). Saint James asks: "What good is it...if someone says he has faith but does not have works?" (James 2:14). Salvation is indeed God's gift, but Jesus teaches that the gift is granted to those who do God's will by keeping the commandments (Matthew 19:17) and by serving others: "Come, you that are blessed by my Father...for I was hungry and you gave me food" (Matthew 25:34-35).

SERVING GOD
THROUGH THE COMMANDMENTS

God made us to know, love, and serve him. When sin made this impossible, Jesus came to take away the sin of the world and bring God's plan back within our reach. His presence in the Church clarifies that plan, shields us from self-deception, and lovingly gives us grace to serve him. We have indeed been blessed by Jesus.

We now look at the Ten Commandments, which show us how to serve God and attain happiness in heaven (Matthew 19:17).

QUESTIONS FOR DISCUSSION AND REFLECTION

Jennifer Fulwider tells how even highly educated people can deceive themselves and justify evils like abortion. What are other examples of such self-deception in today's world? What is the difference between justification and salvation? In what sense do we merit salvation? Read Matthew 25:31–46, Jesus' description of judgment. Does this description agree with the idea that "accepting Jesus as personal Lord and Savior" is all that's necessary for salvation? What does the Church teach about the salvation of those who cannot keep the commandments and serve others because they die in infancy or never achieve mental competence? (Answer: If baptized, they are assured of heaven. And the *Catechism*, number 1261, states that God's mercy and Jesus' tenderness toward children give hope of salvation to such individuals who have died without baptism. For a discussion of this issue, see my book, *The Privilege of Being Catholic*, Liguori Publications, page 129.) Have you ever been asked, "Are you saved?" What is a good way to respond to this question? What is your opinion of the following two answers? 1) "Salvation is my life's journey." 2) "I am working out my own salvation with fear and trembling."

ACTIVITIES

For a more detailed explanation of the concepts touched upon in this chapter, see the *Catechism*, numbers 1987–2051. Meditate on the words of Saint Paul: "For I do not do the good I want, but the evil I do not want is what I do....Wretched man that I am! Who will rescue me from this body of death?" (Romans 7:19, 24). Consider how these words might apply to your life and actions. Ask Jesus to rescue you and all sinners from "this body of death."

CHAPTER 18

The Ten Commandments: Blueprint for an Ideal World

"What would the world be like if everyone kept the Ten Commandments?" I've asked this question of people who wonder why God doesn't do something to make our world better.

God HAS done everything possible to make our world better without taking away our freedom and responsibility as human beings. God has given us a blueprint for an ideal world and that blueprint is the Ten Commandments.

These days it is fashionable in some circles to disparage God's commandments as outdated and restrictive. To see how wrong this is, consider the question that begins this chapter. Answers to the question might include world-wide reverence for the true God, harmony among families, a proper esteem for human life, communication that's always true and kind, respect for the possessions of others, a world without war or crime. This is God's blueprint for an ideal world.

The commandments are not outdated. They were given to humanity by God to bring to every age the peace and joy we long for. Nor are they restrictive. They were designed by God to show us the way to true freedom. If you doubt this, just consider any number of public figures whose lives have been restricted by breaking the commandments.

KNOWING THE TEN COMMANDMENTS

The Ten Commandments are found in the Bible in two separate places, Exodus 20:1–17 and Deuteronomy 5:6–21. The traditional numbering of the commandments as ten is found in the Book of Exodus, which states that Moses stayed with the Lord on Mount Sinai for forty days and nights. "And he wrote on the tablets the words of the covenant, the Ten Commandments" (Exodus 34:28). But the two different listings of the commandments led to diverse ways of counting them. Saint Augustine and most Western Church leaders used the list found in Deuteronomy, as does the Roman Catholic Church today. Saint Jerome and Greek Church leaders followed the Jewish custom of using the Exodus list, and this practice has been maintained by Orthodox and Protestant churches.

Augustine's approach to the commandments led to the traditional catechetical formula quoted in the *Catechism:* 1. I am the Lord your God. You shall not have strange gods before me. 2. You shall not take the name of the Lord your God in vain. 3. Remember to keep holy the Lord's Day. 4. Honor your father and your mother. 5. You shall not kill. 6. You shall not commit adultery. 7. You shall not steal. 8. You shall not bear false witness against your neighbor. 9. You shall not covet your neighbor's wife. 10. You shall not covet your neighbor's goods. (See "The Ten Commandments," in the *Catechism*, preceding *CCC* 2052).

Augustine viewed the directives against making idols (Exodus 20:4–6; Deuteronomy 5:8–11) as an elaboration of the first commandment. Jerome saw these directives as the second commandment: "You shall not make for yourself an idol..." (Exodus 20:4–6). Augustine's second commandment became Jerome's third, the third became the fourth, and so on, until the last two were combined into the tenth: "You shall not covet your neighbor's house; you shall not covet your neighbor's wife, or male or female slave, or ox or donkey, or anything else that belongs to your neighbor." In this, Jerome's list follows Exodus 20:17, which classifies a man's wife with his property. Augustine's list follows Deuteronomy 5:21 in distinguishing the coveting of another's wife (Commandment 9) from the coveting of goods (Commandment 10).

KEEPING THE TEN COMMANDMENTS

The method used for counting the Ten Commandments does not matter as much as keeping them. How important is this? According to Jesus, our eternal happiness depends on it. When asked how to attain eternal life, he replied: "Keep the commandments" (Matthew 19:17).

The Ten Commandments have stood the test of time as standards of morality for countless generations. They deliver us from slavery to sin and make us truly free to follow Christ in keeping the two great commandments which sum up all the rest: "You shall love the Lord, your God, with all your heart, with all your soul, and with all your mind....You shall love your neighbor as yourself" (Matthew 22:37–40).

We aren't likely to keep the commandments if we don't know them. Every Catholic should memorize the Ten Commandments (see page 91) and resolve to keep them. It is true that salvation would be impossible without the life, death, and resurrection of Jesus. It is true that we must put our faith in Jesus. But faith without good works is dead (James 2:17). Jesus tells us, as Chapter 17 noted, that we are saved not by just calling him Lord, but by doing the will of his heavenly Father (Matthew 7:21). Jesus alone is the Way, but the commandments are the road signs that keep us on the Way.

LOVING THE TEN COMMANDMENTS

There is an old joke about Moses coming down from his encounter with God on Mount Sinai and announcing to the Jewish people, "Well, I talked God down to Ten Commandments, but he insists on keeping the sixth and ninth." This bit of humor suggests the attitude that the commandments are burdensome, something to be endured in order to get to heaven. But the real Jewish attitude toward the commandments may be found in Psalm 119, verse 47: "I find my delight in your commandments, because I love them."

We too ought to love God's commandments, treasuring them as we would treasure precious gifts from a good friend. We should spend time in meditation, renewing our love for the Father, Son, and Holy Spirit. In prayer we hear the Father tell us, "With age-old love I have loved you" (Jeremiah 31:3). We hear Jesus say, "You are my friends" (John 15: 14). We meet the Holy Spirit, dwelling within us as a Guest, bringing divine love to us as temples of the Holy Spirit (1 Corinthians 6:19). When we are aware of God's love, we will come to appreciate the commandments as blessings. Keeping them will be no burden, but an act of love. "For the love of God is this, that we obey his commandments. And his commandments are not burdensome...." (1 John 5:3).

THE UNITY AND CONSISTENCY OF GOD'S PLAN

This book addresses life's most basic question: "Why did God make you?" The answer, "to know, love, and serve God in this life and to be happy with Him in the next," is closely linked to the commandments. God's plan has a wonderful unity and consistency. This should be no surprise. God is infinitely wise.

The commandments are connected to knowing God: "Now by this we may be sure that we know him, if we obey his commandments" (1 John 2:3). They are linked to loving God: "If you love me, you will keep my commandments" (John 14:15). They are joined to serving God, for we are called to "...heed his every commandment...loving the Lord your God, and serving him with all your heart and with all your soul" (Deuteronomy 11:13). Finally, the commandments will guide us to being happy forever: "If you want to enter into [eternal] life, keep the commandments" (Matthew 19:17).

In the next chapter, we will begin studying the commandments, one by one. God's blueprint for an ideal world won't be followed by everyone on earth anytime soon. But we can put this blueprint into effect in our own lives, here and now. By doing so, we will make our world as ideal as possible until God calls us to our home in heaven.

QUESTIONS FOR DISCUSSION AND REFLECTION

How would the world change if everyone started keeping the Ten Commandments tomorrow? Have you ever been asked by Protestant friends about our Catholic numbering of the Ten Commandments? Can you explain the reasons behind the differences? Have you ever considered love of the commandments as an important aspect of love of God?

ACTIVITIES

Recite the Ten Commandments from memory. Study the *Catechism's* introduction to the Ten Commandments (CCC 2052–2082). In quiet prayer, reflect on the "unity and consistency of God's plan" shown in the following Scripture passages:

- "Now by this we may be sure that we know him, if we obey his commandments" (1 John 2:3).
- "If you love me, you will keep my commandments" (John 14:15).
- You must "...heed his every commandment...loving the Lord your God, and serving him with all your heart and with all your soul" (Deuteronomy 11:13).
- "If you want to enter into [eternal] life, keep the commandments" (Matthew 19:17).

CHAPTER 19

The First, Second, and Third Commandments

THE FIRST THREE COMMANDMENTS

On January 6, 2009, newspapers around the world reported that German billionaire Adolf Merckle had committed suicide by throwing himself in front of a train. Forbes magazine listed Merckle's net worth at 9.2 billion dollars, but his business interests had run into trouble because of a worldwide financial crisis. While Merckle's worth had dropped from twelve billion dollars two years earlier, he was still one of the wealthiest people in the world. His tragic story underlines a fact many find hard to believe: No amount of money can guarantee happiness and security.

This is an important truth to consider as we begin our study of the commandments. The first commandment proclaims: "I am the Lord your God." We must worship the true God, not false gods. At the time of Moses, people did make idols of gold or silver and worship them. Today we are not likely to fabricate such idols, but we can err by worshiping gold and silver, turning money into a false god. We can make false gods as well of power, pleasure, or popularity.

If so, we are doomed to disappointment. The Book of Ecclesiastes represents Solomon as one who had enjoyed prosperity, power, pleasure, and popularity. But old age found him disillusioned and unhappy: "The words of the Teacher, the son of David, king in Jerusalem. Vanity of vanities, says the Teacher, vanity of vanities! All is vanity" (Ecclesiastes 1:1–2). Only God can satisfy our restless hearts. Only if we worship the one true God, can we find the real meaning and purpose of life. The first three commandments, then, get us off the train tracks of despair and on the way to peace, fulfillment, and happiness.

THE FIRST COMMANDMENT

"I am the Lord your God:
you shall not have strange gods before me."

The first commandment proclaims that there is only one God. We have seen that the one God loves us far more than we can imagine. Jesus teaches us to respond by loving God with our whole being. The first commandment bids us to express our love by adoration, by approaching God with faith, hope, and love. Faith inspires us to believe God and to avoid the sins of willful doubt, unwarranted incredulity, heresy (denial of a truth of faith), apostasy (total repudiation of faith), and schism (separation from the Church's authority). Hope puts our reliance on God, giving us confidence in God's grace and promise of eternal life. It rules out the sins of despair (refusing to trust in God's mercy) and presumption (supposing either that we can save ourselves or that God will save us without effort on our part). Charity summons us to love God above all and to love others for God's sake. Lack of faith, hope, and love can lead to sins such as religious indifference, ingratitude, lukewarmness, spiritual sloth, and hatred of God.

The first commandment orders us to give God what is due by the virtue of religion. This virtue, which guides us in our relationship with God, includes adoration (recognizing God as the Supreme Being), prayer (lifting our minds and hearts to God), and sacrifice (uniting ourselves to Christ's sacrifice). Religion directs us to keep promises to God, especially those made at baptism, confirmation, matrimony, and holy orders. It leads us to seek the truth found in the Catholic Church, and to share that truth with others.

The first commandment forbids the worship of false gods and the sins of superstition, idolatry, divination, magic, irreligion, atheism, and agnosticism. Superstition attributes special powers to actions, objects, or mere external religious practices. Idolatry is the worship of pagan idols, demons, power, pleasure, money, ancestors, the state, or anything that is not God. Divination is the effort to learn the future through astrology, demons, horoscopes or any other supposed power. Magic or sorcery is the attempt to control occult powers in order to help oneself or to help or harm others. Irreligion includes the sins of tempting God (putting God's goodness to the test), sacrilege (profaning anything sacred), and simony (buying or selling spiritual values). Atheism denies that God exists and finds worth only in material things. Agnosticism claims that God cannot be known and often leads to religious indifference.

While the first commandment forbids the making of idolatrous images, it does not forbid all religious images. In the Old Testament, God commanded the creation of the bronze serpent, the ark, the cherubim, and other images to decorate the temple (Exodus 25; Numbers 21; 1 Kings 6–9). The New Testament sees Moses' display of the bronze serpent as a foreshadowing of Christ's being lifted up on the Cross (John 3:14). The Church encourages the veneration of statues and icons of Christ, Mary, the angels, and the saints. These are not idols, but images which honor Christ and the saints, and direct us to true worship of God alone.

THE SECOND COMMANDMENT

"You shall not take the name
of the Lord your God in vain."

In the popular musical, "West Side Story," Tony falls in love with Maria. Enchanted, he sings her name, "Maria." The words herald the beauty of the name. Sung loud, it is music; sung soft, it is prayer.

This song spotlights the respect we have for the name of a loved one. When we come to know and love God, we reverence God's name.

The second commandment tells us to respect God's name, using it to praise and worship God. It teaches us to venerate the name of Jesus, our Lord and God. To appreciate the importance of this commandment, we should relate it to God's love for us and to our love for God. Say the name of God or the name of Jesus with reverence, "...and it's almost like praying."

We wince if we hear someone utter the name of our beloved with contempt. So this commandment forbids disrespectful use of God's name. Blasphemy (words of hatred or defiance against God), cursing, false oaths, perjury, and any other misuse of God's name are sins that scorn God's love. Oaths may be taken in court, but never for trivial or immoral purposes.

Related to a proper reverence for God's name is respect for the name of Mary and names of saints. Their names remind us that God asks us to be saints, calling each of us by name. In response to God's call, we should begin our day, our prayers, and our activities by invoking God as Father, Son, and Holy Spirit in the Sign of the Cross, naming each Person of the Trinity with love.

THE THIRD COMMANDMENT
"Remember to keep holy the Lord's day."

Genesis relates that God rested on the seventh day after the work of creation. This has always been seen by faithful Jews as a pattern for human activity and rest. The Jewish people keep the Sabbath rest on the seventh day of the week (Saturday) to recall their dependence on God and to honor their covenant with God.

Jesus respected the holiness of the Jewish Sabbath, but he also revealed its highest meaning. The Sabbath rest, he taught, must never be used to excuse ourselves from the demands that true love makes. Because Jesus rose from the grave on the first day of the week, we observe Sunday as the Lord's Day, as our Sabbath. We obey the Lord's call to celebrate the Eucharist in memory of him. We gather with our parish community at Mass to express our unity in Christ.

As Catholics, we are obliged to observe the Lord's Day and holy days of obligation by attending Mass. Those who deliberately miss Mass on these days commit a grave sin, unless they are excused by a serious reason. The Church's law also commands us to rest from work or activities that hinder the worship owed to God. Keeping the Lord's Day means devoting time to relaxation, family, works of charity, and concern for the poor and needy. We should consciously give witness to Jesus by our Sunday rest and worship.

FROM THE TRAIN TRACKS OF DESPAIR TO GOD'S WAY

The first three commandments put us confidently on God's way to happiness. The acts of adoring God alone, honoring God's name, and keeping holy the Lord's Day lead us straight to Jesus, who is the Way. He sums up these commandments in the great command to love God with all our heart, mind, and soul. In this love is true happiness, now and forever.

QUESTIONS FOR DISCUSSION AND REFLECTION

What are some examples of worshiping money, power, pleasure, and popularity that you've noticed in real life and in the media? This chapter names many actions that are consistent with keeping the first three commandments. How many can you recall? It lists sins that violate these commandments. How many can you recall? Have you ever been asked about Catholic reverence for statues, perhaps by someone accusing Catholics of idol worship? How have you responded? Have you ever considered the reverent use of God's name as a prayer? Have you been approached by individuals who criticize Christians for worshiping God on Sunday rather than on Saturday? What kinds of work would violate the Sabbath rest? Would these be the same for all? For example, is it a sin for an office worker who enjoys gardening to tend to her garden on Sunday?

ACTIVITIES

A book of this length cannot discuss each commandment in the detail it deserves. For a more detailed study of the first three commandments, consult the *Catechism*, numbers 2083–2195. For New Testament references to Sunday as the day of resurrection and the Lord's Day, see John 20:1, Acts 20:7, 1 Corinthians 16:1–2, and Revelation 1:10.

CHAPTER 20

The Fourth Commandment

"HONOR YOUR FATHER AND YOUR MOTHER."

Mike, a seminarian in Georgia, told me during a parish mission how grateful he is to his father for being such a good Dad and giving him a positive image of God, the Father. At another mission, Jennifer grieved that she couldn't say the Lord's Prayer because her own father had treated her badly. Even the words, "Our Father," brought her pain.

Many people develop positive or negative images of God from their relationships with parents. Perhaps that is why God chose "Honor your father and your mother" as the fourth commandment. The fourth commandment makes the transition from the first three commandments, relating to God, to the remaining seven, relating to people. In a sense, parents are like God to their children. They give life and provide love, food, shelter, and security. When they do this well, they gradually lead their children to know, love, and serve God, the Origin and Source of life, love, and security.

THE EXTENT OF THE COMMANDMENT

The *Catechism of the Catholic Church* notes that children owe parents, after God, honor and respect. The fourth commandment is addressed to children because the bond of children to parents is universal, but it also covers duties to family, relatives, and proper authority. It includes the responsibilities of parents to children and of authorities to those governed.

Saint Paul observes in Ephesians 6:2 that "this is the first commandment with a promise." Deuteronomy 5:16 reads: "Honor your father and your mother, as the LORD your God commanded you, so that your days may be long and that it may go well with you in the land that the LORD your God is giving you." The fourth commandment promises material benefits as well as spiritual blessings. That's because the family is the basic building block of society and the progress of any society depends largely on the strength of its families.

The family was established when God created man and woman and told them to increase and multiply. But one does not have to believe in God to understand the nature and importance of family. Husband and wife join together by matrimonial consent not only for their own good but also for the good of society. Their relationship leads to children, necessary for populating any nation. Children are helpless when they are born and take a long time to mature. They need years of nurturing, guidance, and love. This is why most societies, whether Christian or not, have recognized the importance of the family and have passed laws to protect it.

DUTIES OF CHILDREN AND PARENTS

The duties of children include respect and gratitude for the gift of life. As long as children live in their parents' home they owe them obedience. Children owe obedience also to teachers and others to whom they have been entrusted. Adult children should continue to respect their parents, offering them care and support in old age. Family members should treat one another with love. Believers in Christ should show gratitude to those who brought them the faith.

The command that children must honor parents implies that parents should be honorable. God places a great deal of trust in parents, and they must strive always to be worthy of such trust. Parents should provide for their children's physical and spiritual needs, especially their moral and religious formation. Parents are the first teachers of their children in the ways of faith and should create a home where children can learn Christ's Good News, Christian virtues, and responsibilities toward others. Parents have a right to choose a school corresponding to their own religious convictions, and this right should be protected by civil society.

Parents may advise adult children but must respect their right to choose a spouse and a profession. They should realize that our first vocation is to follow Jesus, and should welcome and nurture God's call to any child to serve Christ in the priesthood or religious life.

THE *CATECHISM,* FAMILY, AND SOCIETY

As the *Catechism* explains, the family, in God's plan, is the original cell of society, essential to society's well-being. The Christian family is a communion of persons, a sign of the unity of Father, Son, and Holy Spirit. The family is a domestic church, a community of faith, hope, and charity, a teacher of moral values and of concern for others, especially the needy. Civil authority should support the family, ensuring its right to exist and to nurture children in peace, dignity, and religious freedom. In a caring society, the family flourishes and shows that all relationships are both personal and familial.

The fourth commandment extends to the duties and rights between civil authorities and citizens. Those in authority must follow the norms of natural law, respect the dignity of citizens, and serve the common good. Citizens should regard legitimate authorities as God's representatives and should promote the well-being of society. They should pay taxes, vote, and defend their country. This last obligation is based on the reality that armed resistance to oppression is sometimes necessary. Those who defend their country in a just war, under the conditions of God's law, are obeying the fourth commandment and deserve our respect and gratitude.

Every society is inspired by a vision of humanity and its destiny. The Catholic Church encourages political authorities to form a vision based on God's revealed truth. While the Church is not linked to any political community, it encourages political freedom and must pass moral judgment on issues involving fundamental human rights and the salvation of souls. God's law is preeminent, and human laws contrary to divine law, such as those promoting abortion and euthanasia, must be opposed and disobeyed. Jesus proclaimed, "Give therefore to the emperor the things that are the emperor's, and to God the things that are God's" (Matthew 22:21).

ATTACKS ON THE FAMILY

In recent decades the family has been under attack. Increasing numbers of babies are born to unwed mothers. More couples are living together outside marriage in liaisons that are notoriously unstable. Many marriages end in divorce. Many agree that these conditions have brought increases in child abuse, broken families, economic hardship, crime, and the prison population.

Further, there is an outcry to recognize "same-sex marriages." We are told that anyone who wants should be able to marry. But if we look at the very nature of marriage, the union of husband and wife who bring forth children for the continuation of society, we can see that redefining marriage to include same-sex liaisons cannot turn these liaisons into marriage. Redefining marriage does not change the nature of marriage. Calling same-sex relationships by the name of marriage does not turn them into the God-designed community that can bring children into the world. But redefining marriage to include such relationships will further devalue marriage and separate humanity from natural law and from God who established this law.

OUR CALL TO STRENGTHEN THE FAMILY

As Catholics, we are called by the fourth commandment to build up marriage and the family. A careful study of the truths outlined in this chapter, truths taught in Scripture and elaborated in the doctrine of the Church, is a good way to begin. Living these truths will strengthen families and bring about a society that is strong and God-centered. When families, the building blocks of society, are healthy, they construct a society that in turn reinforces and supports the family.

"Honor your father and your mother" forms a transition from the commandments relating to God toward those relating to neighbor. It also joins them together. When parents carry out their responsibilities in obedience to the fourth commandment, they encourage their children to obey them. More important, they encourage the children to obey God and live in the Father's love.

QUESTIONS FOR DISCUSSION AND REFLECTION

How has your relationship with your parents affected your relationship with God the Father? Outside your own family circle, who are the best parents you know? What do you most admire about them? It is reported that Abraham Lincoln once asked, "If you call a lamb's tail a leg, how many legs would the lamb have?" When someone answered, "Five," Lincoln said, "The lamb would still have four legs. Calling a tail a leg does not make it a leg." How does this quote apply to present day attacks on marriage? According to the National Center for Health Statistics for the United States, the number of unmarried women who had babies rose from 1,365,966 in 2002 to 1,714,643 in 2007 (www.cdc. gov/nchs/data/databriefs/db18.htm). Children born to unmarried mothers are far more likely to suffer poverty, child abuse, poor education, and other problems. What do these facts say about the importance of good marriages, and about the danger of downgrading the importance of marriage?

ACTIVITIES

You may study this commandment more thoroughly in the *Catechism*, numbers 2196–2257. Consider how your relationship to your father and mother has affected your relationship with God the Father. Ask God to bless your parents, reward them for their good qualities, and forgive them their failings. Ask God the Father to help you trust in his love and overcome any mistrust that might originate in parental failings. The Internet offers sites where you can study organizations that strengthen Catholic marriages. Check out Marriage Encounter at www.wwme.org/ and Retrouvaille at www.retrouvaille.org/.

CHAPTER 21

The Fifth Commandment

"YOU SHALL NOT KILL."

Imelda and Dudley had four children and hoped for a larger family. But after Imelda suffered a miscarriage, her physician recommended that she undergo a hysterectomy. Instead, Imelda and Dudley decided to rely on God's Providence. That was fifty years ago, and the four other children who came along later are grateful to their parents and to God!

More recently, Amy and Chris were told that the child they were expecting had no heartbeat. The physician advised "removal of the non-living tissue." The young parents were not convinced that their child was dead, and they feared that the physician might be suggesting an abortion. They turned to prayer, relying on God's grace and their Catholic faith. The next routine checkup indicated a strong heartbeat, and Amy delivered a healthy baby boy.

Parents like Imelda and Dudley, Amy and Chris, choose life because they believe it is a gift from God. Their children, born out of love and trust, are a blessing to them and to the world.

LIFE: A GIFT FROM GOD

Today, more than ever, humanity must be reminded that life is sacred because it comes from God. The commandment, "You shall not kill," is clarified in another passage, "...do not kill the innocent" (Exodus 23:7). Scripture thus proclaims that it is always evil to murder an innocent person.

Because life is God's gift, we have right to life and to self-defense. In fact, the defense of life is not only a right, but a grave duty for those responsible for the lives of others. As a last resort, parents may use even deadly force to protect children. Police and other legitimate authorities may use arms to protect the innocent.

TODAY'S KILLING FIELDS

Sadly, today's world fails to protect the most innocent of human beings, the unborn. Planet Earth has become a killing field. More human beings are murdered every year than at any point in history. World War II was the most devastating war ever, with a total of perhaps seventy-two million deaths. This averages out at about 12 million annually for the six years of conflict, a ghastly number. But it is dwarfed by the death toll of abortion.

Forty million abortions are performed worldwide every year, according to the Alan Guttmacher Institute, a research wing for Planned Parenthood. Other estimates go as high as fifty million. In six years (the span of WW II), well over two hundred million babies are slaughtered in abortions. Every day, over one hundred thousand human beings are deliberately aborted, more than were killed in the 1945 atomic bombing of Nagasaki. As awful as was World War II, the war on children carried out in today's abortion clinics is far worse.

In our own country, over one million abortions are committed every year. This is more than twice the number of United States soldiers killed in World War II. Never has the statement in the Declaration of Independence, that all are endowed by their Creator with the right to life, been more widely ignored and violated.

Some people attack the Catholic Church and criticize American bishops for their statements about the evil of abortion. It is true that there are other problems in our world. But nothing comes close to the murder of forty million innocents every year. We who are Catholic must become more aware of this culture of death. We must pray, study, speak, and work against it. We must be counter-cultural by showing our respect for life as a gift of God.

SUICIDE, EUTHANASIA, AND THE DEATH PENALTY

Suicide is wrong because it destroys a life that God called into being. It is contrary to love of self and others. Most people who commit suicide do so because of psychological disturbances that diminish their moral responsibility. Only God can weigh the subjective guilt of those who kill themselves out of desperation. The Church commends them to God's mercy and prays for them.

Far different are those who promote suicide as a "lifestyle choice." Organizations like Compassion and Choices (formerly the Hemlock Society), speak of killing human beings as "compassion." Some countries and states have legalized physician-assisted suicide. But planned suicide and euthanasia are not compassion. They destroy God-given life and are mortally sinful.

On the other hand, the Church recognizes that death is not an evil to be avoided at all costs. Just as we can oppose God by destroying innocent life, so we can oppose God by refusing to accept death in God's time. Therefore, medical procedures which are disproportionate to the patient's expected outcome may be declined, and painkillers may be used to alleviate suffering, even at the risk of shortening life. The dying should be given the care necessary to spend their last moments in dignity and peace. Prayer and the sacraments help guide them to God's gift of eternal life.

The death penalty has long been deemed morally acceptable as a way of punishing wicked deeds, deterring crime, and protecting society. However, the Church, following the lead of Pope John Paul II, holds out other options, such as incarceration without possibility of parole. These options deter crime and protect society so that conditions which justify the death penalty are, as John Paul II noted, "very rare, if not practically non-existent" (*Evangelium vitae*, 56).

CARE FOR ONE'S LIFE AND HEALTH

The fifth commandment mandates reasonable care of one's health and prohibits the abuse of food, alcohol, tobacco, drugs, or medicine. Those who seriously endanger others by misuse of drugs or by actions like drunken or reckless driving, commit grave sin.

Medical research must comply with natural law and human dignity. Today there is much public discussion of stem cell potential. Adult stem cell research, which has had many health care applications and shown great promise for the future, is legitimate. Embryonic stem cell research, which involves the killing of a human being, is evil. Embryonic stem cell research has produced no cures and, in the light of recent adult stem cell advances, is difficult to justify even apart from moral considerations.

Genetic embryo screening is a recent development which promises to produce designer babies, but can be grossly immoral. One fertility institute in Los Angeles offered to help couples choose the sex of their baby, as well as eye, hair, and skin color. This is a modern form of eugenics, where imperfect children are discarded. It is estimated, for example, that ninety per cent of Down syndrome babies identified by screening are murdered in the womb. In such cases, the fact that life is a gift of God is ignored, as is the historical reality that other attempts to produce a perfect race, like the attempt of the Nazis in the twentieth century, have ended in disaster.

WAR

Because of human sinfulness, the danger of war is ever present, and governments have the right of legitimate self-defense. Such defense by military force is subject to rigorous conditions traditionally expressed in the "just war" doctrine. Those who serve honorably in the armed forces promote the common good and the cause of peace. Those who refuse to bear arms for reasons of conscience must be allowed to serve their country in some other way. All people should strive to overcome conditions, such as injustice and inequality, which threaten peace.

THE MIND OF CHRIST

Jesus teaches, by word and example, that the fifth commandment forbids any sins hurtful to others, sins such as bullying, psychological and physical abuse, revenge, hatred, unjust anger, prejudice and scandal. These and all sins that fail to see life as God's gift can be conquered if we "have the mind of Christ" (1 Corinthians 2:16). The mind of Christ transforms the fifth commandment and opens hearts and lives to new possibilities: "This is my commandment, that you love one another as I have loved you" (John 15:12).

The fifth commandment, then, leads us, as it led Imelda and Dudley, Amy and Chris, to respect life and to love all others as Christ loves us.

QUESTIONS FOR DISCUSSION AND REFLECTION

Do you know parents like Imelda and Dudley, Amy and Chris, who have made difficult decisions in order to bring new life into the world? Such people challenge a society that badly needs a vision of human life as God's gift. Did you know that unborn wild birds in the United States are protected by law, while the law defends the right of human mothers to kill their unborn babies for any reason? Is God less concerned about human babies than birds? What do such laws say about our society? Have you studied the Church's teaching on stem cell research, especially regarding the distinction between embryonic and adult stem cell research?

ACTIVITIES

Study the fifth commandment in greater detail in the *Catechism*, numbers 2258–2330. Consider this: Those who kill an unborn wild bird in the United States are subject to fines or prison; abortionists who kill unborn human beings are protected by the law and are paid to kill. Pray for our country and pray especially for the conversion of those who promote abortion.

CHAPTER 22

The Sixth and Ninth Commandments

THE SIXTH

"You shall not commit adultery."

Pope Benedict XVI, during his much publicized trip to Africa in March, 2009, said that the AIDS crisis there could not be solved by condoms. He was widely criticized in the media for his statements. But Dr. Edward Green, who oversaw a 2004 survey of AIDS in Africa by the Harvard Center for Population and Development Studies, declared that such criticism of the pope was wrong because the best evidence supports his comments. What is needed is primary behavior change: abstinence before marriage and fidelity after marriage.

Critics of the pope believe that such behavior change is impossible. They say people cannot control themselves. Pope Benedict, following Jesus, believes that people can change their behavior. Jesus and Benedict are right. Statistics show a decline in AIDS, for example, in Uganda where abstinence and fidelity have been emphasized. Elsewhere in Africa, AIDS continues to spread. Those who attack the pope for being out of touch with the modern world are themselves out of touch with reality.

GOODNESS, LOVE, AND SEXUAL MORALITY

The Bible says God created man and woman, telling them to be fruitful and multiply. The sexual nature of human beings, like all of God's creation, is "very good" (Genesis 1:28). But sexual activity causes tragedy if misdirected, so it must be guided by God's laws. The sixth and ninth commandments (Exodus 20:14, 17) forbid genital activity outside marriage. Jesus adds that "everyone who looks at a woman with lust has already committed adultery with her in his heart" (Matthew 5:28). Saint Paul wrote: "Do not be deceived! Fornicators, idolaters, adulterers, male prostitutes, sodomites...none of these will inherit the kingdom of God" (1 Corinthians 6:9–10). Genital sexual activity outside marriage excludes one from God's kingdom.

This is not because sexuality is bad, but because it is so good that it can have its true meaning only in marriage. Sexual intercourse is a means of communication and God wants it to say: "I love you totally, faithfully, forever, with openness to new life. You are the only person I love in this way." But intercourse can say many other things, like "I hate you" in rape, "Let's do business" in prostitution, "Let's seek pleasure but not get serious" in casual sex, or "I think I love you but let's check it out" in a living together arrangement. Such genital sexual activity outside marriage is mortally sinful because it trivializes one of God's greatest gifts.

Some people today may think that such an approach to sexual morality is outmoded. On the contrary, sexual immorality is outmoded. The Greeks of Old Testament times and the pagans of New Testament times wallowed in immorality. Historians like J. D. Unwin have observed that their cultures were destroyed by the erosion of morality. Sexual immorality weakens individuals and families, and when these building blocks of society fail, society itself crumbles.

Tragically, much of the content presented in modern media is controlled by individuals who deride the teachings of Jesus and promote sexual promiscuity. We must have the courage to follow Christ in chastity of body and purity of heart, rejecting the outmoded and hurtful lifestyles glorified in the media.

CHASTITY AND SINS AGAINST THIS VIRTUE

Chastity is the integration of sexuality in one's self and in the gift of self to others. It is the work of a lifetime, involving gradual growth, personal effort, and openness to God's grace. All persons are called to chastity suited to their vocation, conjugal chastity for the married and continence for the unmarried. Sins against chastity include lust, adultery, fornication, pornography, prostitution, rape and masturbation. Homosexual tendencies are not in themselves sinful, but homosexual acts are contrary to natural law and are gravely sinful.

NATURAL FAMILY PLANNING

Human sexuality is ordered toward married love by which husband and wife give themselves to each other for life. Their union achieves the twofold purpose of marriage, the good of the spouses and the transmission of life. Husband and wife are called to imitate God's faithfulness and to follow God's plan that each marriage act be open to the transmission of life. Spouses may plan their family, but their methods must be natural, respecting God's design and avoiding artificial means of contraception.

These days, organic foods and farmers' markets are common, heading a "back to nature" movement that avoids artificial substances. We might suppose that the Church's emphasis on natural family planning would attract favorable attention in this environment. However, natural family planning is more likely to be attacked and ridiculed by the press.

Those who look seriously at natural family planning, like Dr. John Patrick, MD, a Protestant physician and philosopher, sing its praises. Dr. Patrick says that the promised benefits of artificial contraception, such as better marriages and fewer abortions, have failed to materialize. He states that Pope Paul VI, who was viciously attacked for upholding what all churches taught until a few decades ago, was right in promoting the blessings of natural family planning and in predicting the many sad consequences of the contraceptive mentality. Catholic married couples need to understand natural family planning, its effectiveness and its rewards. A good place to begin would be Web sites like www.fertilitycare. org and www.ccli.org.

Children are a blessing from God, and couples who are unable to conceive a baby often suffer real heartbreak. Research aimed at reducing sterility by moral means is encouraged by the Church, and great advances have been made by organizations such as the Paul VI Institute (www.popepaulvi.com). Techniques that require the introduction of third parties by the use of donated sperm or ova are immoral, as are techniques which disassociate the sexual from the procreative.

THE NINTH

"You shall not covet your neighbor's wife."

The ninth commandment forbids sins of lust and carnal concupiscence (desire for sexual gratification contrary to God's will). This commandment brands any intention or desire to commit acts forbidden by the sixth commandment as immoral.

Related issues include attitudes and actions which lead to immoral thoughts and desires. In today's world, pornography is perhaps the devil's most efficient tool for dragging souls into the depths of immorality and ultimately down to the fires of hell. Movies, television, and the Internet, where pornography is a multi-billion dollar business, have lured countless souls into lustful desires, then into actions so shameful and shocking they reek with the stench of hell itself. Anyone addicted to pornography must seek help. A good resource is www.chastity.com.

The ninth commandment directs us to pursue purity of heart, which carries a promise that we shall see God in heaven (Matthew 5:8), and allows us to view others as persons, not objects. Relying on God's grace, we strive for purity by union with Jesus, by the sacraments of Penance and Eucharist, and by prayer. Purity requires modesty, expressed in decency and prudence. It resists immoral excesses in the media, and conquers permissiveness with the Good News of Jesus.

Chastity can be a matter of life or death. In 2008, an Ohio teenager text-messaged a nude picture of herself to her boyfriend. When they broke up, he forwarded the photo to hundreds of teens. The girl became the object of ridicule, sank into depression, and hanged herself in her bedroom. This is an example of how impurity and lust can mingle with modern technology to destroy lives. Catholic moral teaching is indeed up-to-date, in Africa, in the United States, in the bodies and souls of all human beings.

QUESTIONS FOR DISCUSSION AND REFLECTION

Why is sexual immorality outdated? How can we state Catholic teaching on sexual morality in a positive way? How can married couples practice chastity? Why do you suppose that our society praises "getting back to nature," except in the area of natural family planning? How can parents teach children to use modern technology in ways that will help them strive for chastity and union with Jesus?

ACTIVITIES

For a more thorough study of the sixth and ninth commandments, go to the *Catechism*, numbers 2331–2400 and 2514–2533. Pope John Paul II gave a series of lectures on "The Theology of the Body," that shed new light on the meaning of love, marriage, and sexuality. If you would like to learn more about this, a good place to begin would be: www.nfpoutreach.org/Hogan_Theology_%20 Body1.htm. Another option would be to search on the Internet for "Pope John Paul II, Theology of the Body." For an outstanding resource for all issues relating to chastity, including issues like the relationship of the pill to cancer, see www.chastity.com.

CHAPTER 23

The Seventh and Tenth Commandments

THE SEVENTH
"You shall not steal."

There have always been thieves, but in our day, stealing has reached new depths. One Wall Street advisor has been accused of bilking investors out of more than fifty billion dollars. During business failures that caused layoffs of honest workers, some executives voted themselves huge bonuses, partly from tax-paid bailout money. As the old saying goes, "A billion here and a billion there, and pretty soon you're talking about real money."

Though this is a humorous remark, there is nothing funny about the fact that many Americans have lost jobs, health care benefits, and life savings because of the dishonesty of a few greedy individuals. We instinctively know that fraud and greed are wrong. To realize why, we must understand Catholic principles of justice based on the seventh and tenth commandments.

JUSTICE AND GOD'S CREATION

At creation, God entrusted the world to the whole human race. For good reasons, resources have been divided, and people have a right to private property. Because all possessions ultimately come from God, owners should use their belongings with an eye to charity as well as to justice.

Justice, as we've seen in Chapter 15, is a cardinal moral virtue which directs us to give God and others their due. Catholic tradition distinguishes between commutative justice which demands respect for the rights of others, legal justice, which regulates the duties of citizens to the state; and distributive justice which describes the duties of the state to its citizens.

COMMUTATIVE JUSTICE

In the category of commutative justice, the seventh commandment forbids theft, taking the property of another against the reasonable will of its owner. It prohibits deliberate harm to others and their property, including such actions as retaining wages, fraud, abusing credit cards, price fixing, corruption, shoddy work, tax evasion, forgery, false expense accounts, and vandalism. Justice requires restitution when any such harm occurs.

Bets and games of chance are acceptable as long as they do not harm individuals or their family, lead to addiction, or involve cheating. Unfortunately, the spread of gambling casinos in the past few decades has had serious consequences for many individuals and families, and for society as a whole. An article by Maura J. Casey in *First Things* Magazine shows that the presence of casinos has led to increased rates of child neglect, debt, drunken driving, and suicide in the surrounding communities. The seventh commandment calls us to be informed about such issues, to guide our own conduct accordingly, and to bring Christian values to the public square where gambling is involved (www.firstthings.com/article/2009/10/gambling-with-lives).

Cheating is a sin not only in games of chance, but in any life situation where it impinges on the rights of others. Athletes who cheat by using performance-enhancing drugs or by any unfair deception are guilty of stealing victory or team positions from those who follow the rules. Students who cheat in school deprive others of a proper class rank or a scholarship.

The seventh commandment mandates employers to pay an honest wage and to treat workers fairly. It requires workers to give an honest day's work for their wages. It demands that all be faithful in fulfilling contracts and promises.

Any enslavement or trafficking of human beings for profit, a crime all too common in today's world, is immoral. Material resources, plants, and animals are intended by God for human use, but always with concern for the common good and for future generations. While animals may be domesticated or used for food and clothing, they should not be treated cruelly.

DISTRIBUTIVE AND LEGAL JUSTICE

When economic or political issues involve basic human rights or the salvation of souls, the Church applies its social doctrine to relationships between the individual and the state. Catholic social principles, based on Christ's teaching, find unacceptable any system which makes profit the sole norm for economic activity. It rejects the exclusive reliance upon the marketplace that ignores the basic needs of people. It condemns any atheistic ideology associated with communism and socialism, and any system that denies the right to private property.

The Church teaches that work is part of God's plan and can be a means of sanctification. This brings a moral dimension to relationships between workers and employers, which should always be just and fair. Conflicts which arise from economic disparities should be resolved peacefully, by negotiation if possible. Strikes are permissible if necessary to obtain a proportionate benefit. In all arenas of work, lay faithful are called to bring an awareness of God, justice, charity, and solidarity to the marketplace.

The state should guarantee freedom, private property, a stable currency, and public services. It should foster conditions where people have access to employment and a fair wage. Citizens have the obligation to pay just taxes and social security. On the international level, governments must make an effort to reduce the inequities between wealthy and poor nations. Unjust business and financial institutions must be reformed to nurture equitable relationships among nations.

JUSTICE AND THE SPIRITUAL AND CORPORAL WORKS OF MERCY

God calls us to care for people who are poor, and love for them is part of the Church's tradition. We aid poor people through spiritual and corporal works of mercy. The former include instructing, advising, consoling, comforting, forgiving, and bearing wrongs patiently. The latter include feeding the hungry, sheltering the homeless, clothing the naked, visiting the sick and imprisoned, and burying the dead. Almsgiving is a special work of charity and justice. Christ showed compassion for those in misery, and the Church because of a preferential love for the poor, works to bring relief and justice to those in need.

Since all material blessings come from God, we have an obligation to share them with others. We must return to God a portion of what God gives to us. A tradition dating back to Old Testament times suggests we tithe, or give ten percent of our income. The tithe can include our gifts to the Church, the poor, the Catholic education of children, and other worthwhile charities. While the *Catechism* does not mention tithing as a requirement, the sharing of our blessings with the Church and the poor is clearly an obligation of justice. The prophet Malachi (3:8) branded the selfish refusal to share as robbing God.

THE TENTH

"You shall not covet your neighbor's goods."

This commandment forbids craving another's possessions inordinately, and prohibits any deliberate desire to commit actions forbidden by the seventh commandment. It is normal to want good things, and this is acceptable unless it drives us to covet unjustly what belongs to others.

This commandment forbids greed, avarice, and the intention of depriving others of their temporal goods. Envy, which is sadness at another's good fortune or possessions, coupled with an immoderate desire to take these possessions, is a capital sin, mortal if it wishes great harm to the other.

We must battle envy with love, humility, and attentiveness to God, who alone can satisfy our needs. We should appreciate God's free gifts, such as the beauties of nature. Jesus teaches us to choose him over any other good, and never to be seduced by riches. Our great hope must be to see God in heaven. Desire for this true happiness keeps us from excessive attachment to material possessions and frees us for perfect union with God.

JESUS AND A PARABLE ABOUT JUSTICE

In our day, dishonesty has indeed reached new depths. Jesus teaches us to overcome such evil by good. His parable of the Good Samaritan (Luke 10:30–37) displays three attitudes toward justice. The first is that of the robbers who covet the property of others, steal a traveler's belongings, and leave him injured on the roadside. The second is that of the priest and Levite who regard their possessions as theirs alone and refuse to help. The third is that of the Samaritan who sees what he owns as God's gifts and generously shares them with those in need. Jesus points to the Samaritan and tells us, "Go and do likewise" (Luke 10:37).

QUESTIONS FOR DISCUSSION AND REFLECTION

Is it always a sin to take something that belongs to someone else? (For background, see *CCC* 2408). Can you explain in your own words the meaning of commutative, legal, and distributive justice? How does this chapter explain the connection between justice and charity? How well does our country's government approach the goals which justice requires of the state? Is it always a sin to desire possessions that belong to others? If not always sinful, what can make such desires sinful? Which of God's free gifts do you enjoy and appreciate most?

ACTIVITIES

These two commandments are explained in the *Catechism*, numbers 2401–2463 and 2534–2557. The spiritual and corporal works of mercy are listed as given in the *Catechism*, number 2447. An older listing, memorized by many Catholics, may be found at: www.newadvent.org/cathen/10198d.htm. Read the parable of the Good Samaritan, Luke 10:25–37. Ask Jesus to increase in you the virtues of justice and charity.

CHAPTER 24

The Eighth Commandment

"YOU SHALL NOT BEAR FALSE WITNESS AGAINST YOUR NEIGHBOR."

Bishop John Leibrecht of the Diocese of Springfield-Cape Girardeau reported in one of his weekly columns a conversation between two friends. Bill asked, "Have you ever seen one of those lie detector machines that can tell when a man is lying?" "You bet I have," answered Jeff, "I'm married to one."

Perhaps some people can detect truth, but for the whole truth we look to God. Truth is objective reality. Truth is conformity between reality and our expression of it. The Father, source of all that is real, sent his Son, "full of grace and truth" (John 1:14). Jesus is truth (John 14:6), and the Holy Spirit, sent by the Father, is "the Spirit of truth" (John 14:17). We are called as children of God to seek the truth and live in it. We must be witnesses for Jesus to truth in word and deed. We are shown the way to truth and encouraged in this way by the saints, the "great cloud of witnesses" (Hebrews 12:1), especially the martyrs, who gave their lives in witness to Jesus and his truth.

WORDS CAN HURT

There is an Ozark folk tale about a man in the hills who lied so much that somebody else had to call his hounds. The tale expresses the need for truthfulness, and shows that mutual confidence among human beings (dogs too!) is necessary for social relationships. If people cannot trust one another, social interaction is impossible.

Therefore, the eighth commandment forbids false statements of every kind. Due to the importance of public declarations in court, false witness and perjury under oath are sins of special gravity. If they lead to the condemnation of innocent people, the exoneration of the guilty or serious harm of any kind to others, they are gravely sinful, and the witness is bound in conscience to retract any false statements.

Respect for truth and the reputation of others forbids rash judgment (presuming fault in another without sufficient reason), detraction (disclosing another's faults without good cause), and calumny (telling lies about another). Such sins are common in today's society, and they all fit into the category of gossip, which is report or rumor, often negative, about the conduct of others.

We can trick ourselves into thinking that hurtful gossip is not a sin. We can disguise it as sympathy: "It's awful how that poor woman has been treated by her cheating husband." We can pose it as a question: "Have you heard about the problems that couple is having?" Humorists say that in the South it's okay to express any gossip as long as you close with, "Bless his heart." "He's so ugly he could make a train take a dirt road, bless his heart."

But cruel and hurtful remarks are not to be taken lightly, nor is gossip of any kind. Jesus said, "Do not judge, so that you may not be judged. For with the judgment you make you will be judged, and the measure you give will be the measure you get" (Matthew 7:1–2). At the time of judgment, many of us will find ourselves wishing we had spoken more kindly of others.

HARMFUL SPEECH

Honesty prohibits flattery, adulation (phony praise), boasting, harmful irony, and lying. Lying is defined as speaking falsehood with the intention of deceiving those who have a right to the truth.

The gravity of this sin depends on the harm done, and lies become mortally sinful when they cause grave harm to another.

Reparation must be made for offenses against truth, to the extent that this is possible. Anyone guilty of calumny is obliged to correct false statements and to undo any harm caused by them. This can be difficult in the case of calumny and of detraction as well. Saint Philip Neri is said to have given money to a woman with a wicked tongue, instructing her to go to the market, buy a slaughtered chicken, and bring it to him, plucking its feathers on the way. When she returned with the chicken, he told her to go back and pick up all the feathers. "That's impossible," she replied. "The wind has scattered them everywhere." "Yes," he said, "and your hurtful words have been scattered everywhere by those who hear and repeat your gossip." It may be difficult to repair all the damage done by gossip, but we should apologize for any harm done, speak well of those we might have hurt, and pray for victims of unkind speech.

Being Discreet

In some cases, people who seek information have no right to it. Here charity and respect for truth may require silence or discreet language. We are not required to tell the truth to someone who has no right to know it.

Some years ago, a grandmother told me about her granddaughter's first confession. Mom was sitting near her daughter as she waited her turn. Mom asked if she had her sins ready to confess, and the child said she had only four. She had fought with her little brothers, got angry, disobeyed, and lied. So Mom asked whom she had lied to, and she said, "I lied to my Mommy and Daddy." Mom got a bit too curious and asked what she had lied about. The girl looked Mom right in the eye and said, "I'll tell the priest, but I won't tell you."

Priests may never violate the seal of confession under any

circumstance or for any reason. Professional secrets, like those of doctors, lawyers, and soldiers, must be kept, except in cases where to do so would cause very grave harm to the one who confided it, to the one who received it, or to an innocent third party.

When someone inquires about information to which they have no right or which might seriously harm another, we may use the technique known as mental reservation. A close friend might tell you about a serious problem, trusting you to keep it a secret. Someone else asks, "Do you know anything about this?" You may legitimately reply, "No, I don't." Implied are the words (the mental reservation), "I don't know anything that I'm free to tell others."

MEDIA, ART, TRUTH, AND BEAUTY

All people should respect the private lives of others. Today's world seems to have lost sight of this fact. There are gossip magazines at checkout counters, and Internet sites that spread rumors and harmful reports. While those in the media have a responsibility to dispense news, they must do so with concern for the common good and with a proper respect for the rights of individuals.

God's truth is beautiful. It is revealed in created things and in the words of Scripture, and we should seek the beauty in them. This beauty can and should be expressed in art, especially sacred art, which evokes the mystery and grandeur of God. Genuine art draws us to adoration, prayer, and love of God, and we should seek God in all that is beautiful and true.

THE PRECEPTS OF THE CHURCH

Chapter 17 stated that Jesus gave us the Church to teach us what the commandments mean and to guide us in keeping them. Now that we have concluded our study of the Ten Commandments, we should consider the Precepts of the Church. These are traditional guidelines that are meant to establish the indispensable minimum for Christian moral life. The five precepts listed in the *Catechism*, numbers 2041–2043, are as follows: 1) You shall attend Mass on Sundays and on holy days of obligation and rest from servile labor. 2) You shall confess your sins at least once a year. 3) You shall receive the sacrament of the Eucharist at least during the Easter season. 4) You shall observe the days of fasting and abstinence established by the Church. 5) You shall help to provide for the needs of the Church.

We don't need lie-detector machines when we look to God for truth and for the true way to serve God. We find both in the Ten Commandments and in the Church.

QUESTIONS FOR DISCUSSION AND REFLECTION

Some have said that because gossip and lying are so common, the eighth commandment is broken more than any other. Do you agree? What is your opinion of this statement: "Great minds discuss ideas, good minds discuss events, and weak minds discuss people"? In what way is someone's choosing to share gossip with you actually a negative judgment on your character? Can you think of situations where mental reservation is justified? Of situations where it is not justified? What kinds of art and music tend to open you to God's truth and beauty?

ACTIVITIES

You may study the eighth commandment in the *Catechism*, numbers 2464–2513. For a history of the precepts of the Church and a list of the precepts as given in the *Baltimore Catechism*, see: www. newadvent.org/cathen/04154a.htm. In prayer, place yourself in God's presence. Recall the Ten Commandments one by one and consider how each is a sign of God's love for you and for the world.

CHAPTER 25

Getting Personal With God

Stan and Christy were expecting their second child, but Christy suffered a miscarriage. Bill lost his job unexpectedly. Henry was diagnosed with terminal cancer, only a few months after his son had died of cancer. Sheila, just fifty-five years of age, is confined to a nursing home, where she is trying to regain mobility and speech after a severe stroke.

Stan, Christy, Bill, Henry, and Sheila are believers who are active in the practice of the Catholic faith and do their best to keep the commandments. But living one's faith and keeping the commandments will not guarantee a life of comfort and ease. Nor will striving to know, love, and serve God. Our world has been touched by sin. Good people suffer. Jesus never promised believers a life of comfort and ease. On the contrary, he said, "If any want to become my followers, let them deny themselves and take up their cross daily and follow me" (Luke 9:23).

But people who seem to have everything the world can give will suffer too. Consider Elvis Presley and Michael Jackson. Both had great talent, wealth, and fame. Both died in circumstances that made their deaths seem tragic and pointless.

To know, love, and serve God by keeping the commandments is never tragic, never pointless. Christy, for example, related how God had brought peace through the knowledge that she would be with her child forever. Bill, Henry, and Sheila found strength in God's presence and love.

Keeping the commandments doesn't promise comfort and ease, but it does promise something better. "If you want to enter into life, keep the commandments" (Matthew 19:17). This promise of Jesus refers to eternal life. It is also a promise of abundant life here and now.

This abundant life is the life of love, love that is linked with keeping the commandments, love that brought joy to Jesus even in the face of horrible suffering. "As the Father has loved me, so I have loved you; abide in my love. If you keep my commandments, you will abide in my love, just as I have kept my Father's commandments and abide in his love. I have said these things to you so that my joy may be in you, and that your joy may be complete" (John 15:9–11).

To live in love and joy, we must get personal with God. God is three Persons: Father, Son, and Holy Spirit. Let's look again at each Person, this time with our focus on how we may draw strength and courage from our friendship with Father, Son, and Holy Spirit.

THE FATHER

The Father is Creator of the universe, who guides all with his Providence. This means that nothing can happen unless the Father wills or allows it. The distinction between "willing" and "allowing" is important because the Father never wills anything evil. We've seen how human beings must be free to be capable of love. They can make sinful choices that harm themselves and others. God does not will those sinful choices, but allows them for the sake of freedom. When a child is killed by a drunken driver, this is not God's will. But God is not absent. God is there to bring the child through death to eternal life. God is present to give comfort and strength to the child's parents, guiding them to hope and peace. God is near to call the drunk driver to repentance and restitution. All involved in such tragedies are invited to turn to God the Father and trust in his Providence.

Jesus himself leads those who are heavily burdened to the Father, and promises them rest (Matthew 11:25–30). Saint Paul assures the faithful who struggle that God will bring victory:

"No, in all these things we are more than conquerors through him who loved us. For I am convinced that neither death, nor life, nor angels, nor rulers, nor things present, nor things to come, nor powers, nor height, nor depth, nor anything else in all creation, will be able to separate us from the love of God in Christ Jesus our Lord" (Romans 8:37–39).

THE SON

Jesus came into our world to share every aspect of human life, good and bad, except sin. A key to surviving any difficulty is to think, speak, and act like Jesus. Learning to do this is the work of a lifetime. The more we ponder the New Testament, the more we'll be able to put on "the mind of Christ" (1 Corinthians 2:16). A good place to begin is the Sermon on the Mount (Matthew 5–7), where Jesus takes us beyond the commandments to the very heart of God.

But as we try to put on the mind of Christ, we'll find Bible passages that are difficult and disconcerting. "Do not resist an evildoer. But if anyone strikes you on the right cheek, turn the other also; and if anyone wants to sue you and take your coat, give your cloak as well; and if anyone forces you to go one mile, go also the second mile" (Matthew 5:39–41). Is Jesus saying that a husband should do nothing while an intruder slaughters his wife and children? That a woman robbed of her purse should pursue the thief to give up her watch? That a physician should spend hours listening to the complaints of a person with hypochondria instead of doing scheduled surgery?

Not at all. To discover what Jesus means, we must realize that any biblical passage is to be understood in light of the whole Bible. In Matthew 5:39–41, Jesus is saying that people are more important than insults (the slap), property (the coat and cloak), and time (walking the extra mile). There are occasions when we should overlook insults, share possessions, and offer our time to help others.

But there are situations when we must confront evildoing, guard our property, and walk away from those who waste our time. Jesus did not turn the other cheek when slapped by a temple officer (John 18:23). Jesus drove out thieving money-changers from the temple (Matthew 21:12–13). Jesus did not walk the extra mile to please Herod Antipas, and when arrested and brought before Herod, Jesus refused to speak to him (Luke 9:9; 23:9).

When should we suffer in silence and when should we confront evildoing? The answer is found in judging what the most loving thing to do is, what is best for the other. This may mean acceptance in one case and confrontation in another.

Difficult passages become understandable when we view them in the context of the whole Bible. They find meaning in the teaching of the Church, guided by the Holy Spirit. As we come to know Jesus by study and prayer, we'll want to do more than keep the commandments. We'll want to think, speak, and act like Jesus.

THE HOLY SPIRIT

Jesus sends us the Holy Spirit as Advocate, as Helper (John 14:26). At every moment, in any difficulty, the Holy Spirit is present to help us. My own friendship with the Holy Spirit is nourished by two simple practices. The first is to pray frequently a favorite Scripture verse: "The Spirit God gives is no cowardly spirit, but One that makes us strong, loving, and wise" (see 2 Timothy 1:7). The second is to recall the fruits of the Holy Spirit. As mentioned earlier, nine are listed in Galatians 5:22–23. I consider how each is evident in the life of Jesus and ponder how I can depend on the Holy Spirit to let each fruit find expression in my life.

The fruit of the Spirit is everywhere evident in the life of Jesus. Love shines through when Jesus takes children in his arms and blesses them (Mark 10:13–16). Joy is present even as he faces suffering and death (John 15:11). Peace is a gift he offers a world intent on his destruction (John 14:27). Patience is his response to persecution, even after his Ascension into heaven (1 Timothy 1:16). His kindness eases the pain endured by others (Luke 7:12–15). Generosity marks his every moment on earth, to the point of shedding his blood (John 19:34). His faithfulness to friends, even when they are faithless, illuminates the dark night of his arrest (John 18:8). Gentleness characterizes his relationships toward all, as when from the cross he forgives his enemies (Luke 23:34) and attends to the needs of his Mother (John 19:26–27). Self-control restrains his divine power from destroying his enemies (Luke 4:16–30; Matthew 26:50–53). Reflecting on the fruits of the Spirit in the life of Jesus can help this fruit flourish in us.

GETTING PERSONAL WITH GOD MAKES US STRONG, LOVING, AND WISE

The Spirit God gives is one that makes us strong with the creative, providential power of God the Father, the love of Jesus, and the wisdom of the Holy Spirit. To paraphrase Saint Paul in Romans 8:31: "If such a mighty, loving, wise God is for us, who can be against us?"

QUESTIONS FOR DISCUSSION AND REFLECTION

Do you know people who have suffered great hardships and yet stayed close to Jesus? What do you think has been the source of their strength? How has the Father's Providence been evident in your life? Do you find the explanation of Jesus' saying to turn the other cheek helpful? How often in a typical day do you turn to the Holy Spirit for strength, love, and wisdom?

ACTIVITIES

Take time to quiet yourself in prayer. Then consider each fruit of the Spirit (love, joy, peace, patience, kindness, generosity, faithfulness, gentleness, and self-control). Think of ways, in addition to those listed above, in which each fruit is expressed in the life of Jesus. Ask Jesus to help you imitate him by making you more conscious of the Holy Spirit's presence within you. Peacefully recite these words: "The Spirit God gives is no cowardly spirit, but One that makes us strong, loving, and wise" (see 2 Timothy 1:7). Notice how "strong, loving, and wise" can relate to serving, loving, and knowing God.

CHAPTER 26

Spirituality 101

everal years ago, my high school class celebrated its fiftieth anniversary of graduation. At a gathering of classmates, I remarked that it took us longer to get from first to eighth grade than from eighth grade to today. No one disagreed. We go from seven to seventy in only a moment.

What matters is that as we grow in years we grow also in spirituality and holiness. Some time ago I was discussing the content of this book with friends Rob and Sallie. Rob said, "You should include a chapter on how to make progress in holiness, getting from kindergarten to graduate school in the spiritual life. You could call it, 'Small Steps for the Spiritual Walk with Christ' or 'Spirituality 101.'" I asked Rob and Sallie, who love and live their Catholic faith, for ideas on Spirituality 101. Their suggestions are the basis of this chapter.

SCRIPTURE AND THE *CATECHISM*

Sallie said, "It is important to emphasize knowledge of God through Scripture and Church teaching." That places an exclamation point behind the first part of this book: "God made me to know him!" It is not enough to know about God. We must know God.

In Chapters 4, 5, and 25, we saw how God invites us to know him as a friend. There is an exciting, awesome challenge here. The Old Testament says that Moses was so intimate with God that "...the Lord used to speak to him face-to-face, as one speaks to a friend" (Exodus 33:11). Yet, just a few verses later, Exodus relates that God tells Moses: "...you shall see my back; but my face shall not be seen" (33:23). The author of Exodus was certainly aware of the conflict implied in these verses. He wants us realize that knowing God, seeing God face to face, is veiled in mystery.

After Jesus was born, people could see God face-to-face, as the Apostle Thomas did when he adored the risen Christ: "My Lord and my God" (John 20:28). We, on the other hand, are among those of whom Jesus said, "Blessed are those who have not seen and yet have come to believe" (John 20:29).

We come to believe in Jesus through Scripture. John says, "Now Jesus did many other signs in the presence of his disciples, which are not written in this book. But these are written so that you may come to believe that Jesus is the Messiah, the Son of God, and that through believing you may have life in his name" (John 20:30–31).

If you are not an avid reader of the Bible, you should be! If your parish offers Bible study, you might begin there. Or you might use *A Catholic Guide to the Bible* (Liguori Publications) as an introduction to the Bible. But don't wait. Begin reading the Bible today, using the Gospel of Luke as a starting point, followed by the Acts of the Apostles and Paul's Letter to the Philippians.

Rob suggests making a resolution you can keep about the amount of reading involved: Read a paragraph a day. Soon you'll begin to see the Bible as God's love letter to you, and you'll want more of God's word and love to light up your life.

Chapter 14 noted the importance of the *Catechism* as a resource for Catholics. The *Catechism* can be read cover-to-cover, and it can be used as a reference work. Either way, it will lead us to a deeper knowledge of our Faith and to a closer friendship with Jesus.

THE SACRAMENTS

God speaks to us through Scripture. God is present to us in the sacraments. We want to spend time with friends, and Jesus gave us the sacraments so that he might be with us, and we with him.

Rob and Sallie put the sacraments on top of their list of important ways to grow in the spiritual life. So does Jesus.

Baptism makes us children of the Father, brothers and sisters of Jesus, temples of the Holy Spirit, and members of the Church that is Christ's body on earth. Confirmation strengthens our relationship with the Father, draws us closer to Jesus, opens us more profoundly to the Holy Spirit, and intensifies our bond with the Church. These sacraments are received only once, but the blessings they bring, such as the virtues of faith, hope, and charity and the gifts of the Holy Spirit, remain with us. Spiritual growth means that we become more aware of such blessings and share them with others.

The Eucharist is, the *Catechism* tells us, "the source and summit of the Christian life," (CCC 1324) because the Eucharist IS Jesus Christ. At Mass Jesus leads us in prayer, speaks to us through Scripture, and nourishes us with his Body and Blood, his very self. Holy Communion unites us to Jesus, making us one with him. Spirituality means union with God, and there is no closer union with God than Holy Communion. Jesus said, "Those who eat my flesh and drink my blood abide in me, and I in them" (John 6:56).

God tells us to attend Mass on the Lord's Day. Rob and Sallie recommend daily Mass and Holy Communion when possible. I am privileged to celebrate Mass every day, and I can say without hesitation that this is the greatest blessing in life. I've been impressed with the devotion of young and old who attend Mass and receive Holy Communion frequently. Such people know the power of the Eucharist, and how participation in the Mass allows them to say with Saint Paul that "...it is no longer I who live, but it is Christ who lives in me" (Galatians 2:20).

We are given new life in baptism and confirmation, and we are united to Jesus in the Eucharist. But we are sinners. We need forgiveness. Jesus forgives. On the greatest evening of his life, Easter Sunday evening, Jesus appeared to the Apostles and said to them, "Receive the Holy Spirit. If you forgive the sins of any, they are forgiven them; if you retain the sins of any, they are retained"

(John 20:22–23). Through the sacrament of penance, Jesus makes it clear that he is never distant or impersonal. We confess our sins to Jesus in this sacrament, and Jesus is there to tell us, person to person, that our sins are forgiven. By his grace, Jesus turns what might seem a roadblock, our sinfulness, into an opportunity for new closeness to God. We ought to approach this sacrament frequently, for in it we meet the forgiving Christ.

The sacraments of matrimony and holy orders promise special sacramental graces to those who receive them. By reason of their baptism and confirmation, vowed religious and lay people dedicated to serve God as committed single Catholics can count on Christ's grace and blessings as they follow him. All Catholics receive assurance in the anointing of the sick that Jesus will bring the healing that God wills and will finally raise them to eternal life.

PRAYER

Rob and Sallie are members of a parish that sponsors perpetual adoration of the Blessed Sacrament. They agree with what Chapter 8 states about the beauty and power of adoration. They also encourage many classic forms of Catholic prayer, forms which are sometimes overlooked. These forms include the morning offering, meal prayers, praying with children and blessing them. Additional classic forms of prayer include saying a prayer for safety when beginning a trip, praying the rosary while traveling (Rob keeps a finger rosary in his car to use while driving to and from work), a prayer to Saint Anthony when something is lost, and the nightly examination of conscience followed by an act of contrition. Rob and Sallie suggest also making a list of names of friends who request prayers. Such people can be remembered at Mass and adoration, while praying the rosary, and at other prayer times.

Rob has begun saying the Liturgy of the Hours, the Church's official prayer offered daily by priests, deacons, and religious. Many lay people say this prayer, and some parishes schedule Morning and Evening Prayer on a regular basis. You can find this prayer on the Internet in several formats through an Internet search for "Liturgy of the Hours."

OTHER RECOMMENDATIONS

Additional recommendations for spiritual growth include regular spiritual reading, works of penance such as fasting and abstinence (especially from things that are harmful to one's health), and offering up one's sufferings for others.

An important help to growth in holiness is spiritual direction. In today's busy world, however, it can be difficult to find competent spiritual guides. Many Catholics receive direction and guidance through programs like Cursillo (www.natl-cursillo.org), Teens Encounter Christ (www.tecconference.org), Life Teen (www.lifeteen.com), and Franciscan University Summer Conferences (www.franciscanconferences.com and www.franciscanyouth.com). Other Catholic institutions that promote holiness and apostolic life among lay people include Opus Dei (www.opusdei.us) and Regnum Christi (www.regnumchristi.org).

Finally, both Rob and Sallie stressed the importance of actively working in some ministry of service and evangelization. A good place to begin is your parish. Jesus calls us into the Church to be apostles, to bring the Gospel and the love of Christ to the world.

TIMES AND CIRCUMSTANCES

Rob suggests that we structure Spirituality 101 according to times and circumstances of life. There are special opportunities for spiritual growth, for example, when a young couple is married. Parents pray with small children and learn with them as they lead the children through sacramental preparation. When children become involved in sports, parents pray for their safety and teach by word and example how faith leads to sportsmanship and humility in winning and to graciousness in losing. There are new reasons for prayer when children reach adolescence and the high school years. An empty nest can offer husband and wife more time together for Bible study, prayer, daily Mass, and eucharistic adoration. The marriage and other vocational choices of children will present occasions for prayer and spiritual growth. Grandparents can pray with grandchildren, help teach them the faith, and encourage them to follow Jesus. Old age leads to a better understanding of how this life is meant to lead us to know, love, and serve God as we move closer to happiness with God in heaven.

Through all the decades of life, our aim should be to know Jesus, to think, speak, and act like Jesus. As we grow spiritually, the more we practice virtue, the easier it becomes to "put on the Lord Jesus Christ" (Romans 13:14), and to pass from the baby steps of spiritual childhood to real spiritual growth, until we "... come to the unity of the faith and of the knowledge of the Son of God, to maturity, to the measure of the full stature of Christ" (Ephesians 4:13).

Life on earth goes by quickly. Spirituality 101 helps us find the life that lasts forever!

QUESTIONS FOR DISCUSSION AND REFLECTION

Has time gone by more quickly for you as you have grown older? For many people, time seemed to pass more slowly when we we're young. Why do you think this is so? Of the suggestions for spiritual growth mentioned in this chapter, which seem the most valuable to you? Why? Which of the recommendations seem most difficult? Why? What are some practical steps you can take to grow in knowledge and love of God? If progress in the spiritual life begins in "spiritual kindergarten" and concludes with graduation from "spiritual graduate school," in what grade would you place yourself at this time?

ACTIVITIES

Try "spiritual cross-training." See *The Search for Happiness, We Worship: A Guide to the Catholic Mass*, and *We Pray: Living in God's Presence* for three approaches to spirituality.

Take time to be with Jesus in prayer. Listen as he tells you, "I am with you always" (Matthew 28:20). Go through the decades of your life, considering how God has called you to spiritual growth each step along the way. Pray for the grace to "...come to the unity of the faith and of the knowledge of the Son of God, to maturity, to the measure of the full stature of Christ" (Ephesians 4:13).

CHAPTER 27

Assurance Here and Hereafter

W oody Allen is a comedian, actor, and movie producer. He is also an atheist, but he makes an interesting observation about people who believe in God:

> *If you actually have faith, if you believe that there's something more to life in a positive sense, then of course it's a wonderful, wonderful thing. But I just can't bring myself to do it. If I'm sitting next to a guy and he has true belief, I look at him and think, poor thing, you really are deluded. But his life is much better than mine.*
>
> READER'S DIGEST, SEPTEMBER, 2008

ASSURANCE HERE

Woody Allen thinks believers are deluded, even as he admits their lives are much better than his. But delusions do not make anything better. Delusions don't work in the real world. If you're not sure whether the top or bottom switch turns on the light, you can try both. When the light comes on, you've clicked the right switch. When the switch marked "belief" turns on the light of meaning and happiness in life, you have good reason to know it is real. Former atheists find meaning in life when they turn to belief, when they begin to know, love and serve God. Lights come on. Belief is real, not a delusion.

As a practical application, we might consider the results of believing in God and keeping the commandments. If God is a delusion, it's difficult to imagine, for example, that going to church, keeping holy the Lord's Day, would have positive consequences. But it does, indicating that God is no delusion.

Studies completed at Duke University in 1999 show that regular church attendance is good for our physical, emotional, and mental health. The effect of regular worship on survival is equivalent to that of wearing seat belts versus not wearing them in auto accidents, and of not smoking versus smoking (Duke University Center for the Study of Religion, www.dukespiritualityandhealth.org).

A study of five hundred fifty adults by psychology professor Susan Lutgendorf of the University of Iowa revealed that attending church at least once a week increases a person's chances of living longer by 35%. Church attendees also have lower blood pressure and stronger immune systems. Robert Wallace, a coauthor of the study, said doctors could prescribe church attendance to benefit patients! (www.washingtontimes.com/news/2004/dec/26/20041226-104514-3168r/).

Dr. Daniel Hall, MD conducted a study at the University of Pittsburgh Medical Center indicating that regular church attendance can add two to three years of life. Dr. Hall noted that the effects of church attendance were similar to using cholesterol-lowering medications, but without the cost (www.jabfm.org/cgi/content/abstract/19/2/103).

These studies do not try to explain why regular church attendance has such positive advantages for health and longevity. But we can safely assume that such studies are at the very least a good reason to take God seriously.

We should look also at another controversial modern issue relating to knowing, loving, and serving God: sexual morality. Today's world, as we noted in Chapter 22, tends to mock the notion of chastity. Promiscuity is glorified in the media and on college campuses. What brings true happiness and satisfaction, however, is not promiscuity, but observance of God's law.

An article in *USA Today* on February 12, 1999, by William

R. Mattox, Jr., was titled, "Aha! Call It Revenge of the Church Ladies." The article cited comprehensive research showing that people who follow the standards of biblical morality and the teachings of Jesus are the ones who find satisfaction and real happiness in their relationships. The article is worth reading and can be found at www.crossroadschristianfellowship.org/biblestudy/revengeofthechurchladies.pdf.

We should consider such research as we study life's meaning and the rewards of serving God. Some people ridicule believers and glorify immorality. We can be intimidated by their arrogance and their contempt for our faith. Yet, the reality is that such people ignore facts or try to explain them away, as Mary Eberstadt shows in "The Will to Disbelieve," *First Things*, February 2009. This article, well-documented and fascinating, may be found at www.articlearchives.com/education-training/students-student-life/2304099-1.html.

While some may disbelieve, we must be counted among those who know, love, and serve God. Elements in today's culture may lead people to doubt God's existence and disparage Christian morality. Church attendance is down, in spite of evidence that regular attendance is good for us. Immorality is praised in spite of evidence showing how it harms individuals and society. We must be counter-cultural, following Jesus and bringing him, and a better life, to others. The evidence supports us in this mission!

ASSURANCE HEREAFTER

We should find assurance in evidence that affirms the benefits of keeping the commandments relating to God and neighbor. This is assurance here and now for our efforts to follow Jesus. There is more assurance in heaven, our "hereafter."

We are not the first believers to see a downturn in Mass attendance and to be persecuted by the secular world. When Jesus preached his first sermon on the Eucharist (John 6), most of his listeners walked away. Jesus was persecuted by the world and put to death on the cross. He warned his followers, "If they persecuted me, they will persecute you" (John 15:20).

Soon after the resurrection, there were believers who stopped attending the liturgical assembly, the Eucharist (Hebrews 10:25). Christians were reminded that "...you endured a hard struggle with sufferings, sometimes being publicly exposed to abuse and persecution... and you cheerfully accepted the plundering of your possessions" (Hebrews 10:33–34).

The inspired author of Hebrews found assurance in the great heroes who had been faithful to God in the past and now watched over believers from heaven (Hebrews 11). He told the Christians who struggled with temptations to discouragement and doubt:

> *Therefore, since we are surrounded by so great a cloud of witnesses, let us also lay aside every weight and the sin that clings so closely, and let us run with perseverance the race that is set before us, looking to Jesus the pioneer and perfecter of our faith, who for the sake of the joy that was set before him endured the cross, disregarding its shame, and has taken his seat at the right hand of the throne of God.*
>
> HEBREWS 12:1–2

From New Testament times, believers have been looking to the hereafter for assurance, strength, and courage. God says to us through Scripture: "Remember your leaders, those who spoke the word of God to you; consider the outcome of their way of life, and imitate their faith" (Hebrews 13:7).

In obedience to God's word, we remember our leaders, the Apostles. They abandoned Jesus before his crucifixion, but boldly proclaimed him as Lord and Savior after his resurrection. They had nothing to gain from this except persecution, torture, and martyrdom. Yet not one of the apostles renounced Jesus or claimed that they had invented the account of the resurrection even though this would have saved their lives. The only explanation for this courage is that they had indeed seen the risen Christ.

Through the centuries, countless martyrs have imitated the Apostles and gladly given their lives for Christ. Saint Ignatius of Antioch was arrested in 107 by Roman authorities and brought to Rome in chains to be fed to the lions in the arena. On the way, he wrote to Christians in Rome, saying he longed to be the "food of lions" and to be "pure bread" ground by their teeth for Christ. Father Thomas Somers and Father John Roberts ministered to persecuted Catholics in England under King James I. They were captured by the authorities in 1610 and sentenced to a slow, horrible death by being hanged, drawn, and quartered. On the night before their execution, Luisa de Carvajal, a Spanish noblewoman, bribed the jailor to let her provide dinner for the two priests and other imprisoned Catholics. The two martyrs were so joyful that Father Roberts even apologized to Luisa that perhaps he was "causing disedification" by his "great glee" (*Magnificat*, Dec. 2003, Vol. 5, No. 10, Page 143).

Father Theophane Venard was a missionary martyred in Viet Nam in 1861 after months of confinement and torture. The executioner asked Father Venard what he would give to be killed quickly. Father Venard, seeing his martyrdom as an act of witness to Jesus, replied, "The longer it lasts, the better."

These martyrs, and others beyond numbering, give proof of Christ's presence and power even at the worst of times. They show, as Paul promised, that neither death "nor anything else in all creation, will be able to separate us from the love of God in Christ Jesus our Lord" (Romans 8:39). When we are tempted to discouragement or self-pity by the defection of believers or the scorn of non-believers, we should call to mind the martyrs, this "great cloud of witnesses," and "run with perseverance the race that is set before us" (Hebrews 12:1). Woody Allen is right about one important thing. Believers do have a better life. The evidence is everywhere, here and hereafter!

QUESTIONS FOR DISCUSSION AND REFLECTION

What is your reaction to Woody Allen's statement quoted at the beginning of this chapter? How would you respond to him? Studies show that regular Sunday worship is good for your physical, mental, and emotional health, and that people who follow Christian standards of morality are happier in their marriages. Do the results of such studies surprise you or would you expect them? Why? Do you have any favorite saints whose lives and heroism give you strength and hope? Where do the martyrs get the courage to face torture and death with such peace and joy?

ACTIVITIES

Judas betrayed Jesus, and the early Church suffered from dissension and strife. Read, for example, Paul's words to the elders of Ephesus (Acts 20:29–30). Read also 2 John 7–11 and 3 John 9–10, and consider how Jesus has delivered the Church from such problems throughout the history of his Church. Ask him to protect and guide his Church always.

Reading the lives of saints can inspire us to follow Christ more faithfully as we "imitate their faith" (see Hebrews 13:7). Many parishes offer calendars that list the saints honored at weekday Masses. An Internet search for the names of these saints or for patron saints will bring up much information about them. Try this with some of your favorite saints.

CHAPTER 28

To Be Happy
With God Forever

Some years ago, Bishop John Leibrecht of the Diocese of Spring-field-Cape Girardeau visited an elderly priest, Father Val, who was hospitalized and critically ill. When Bishop Leibrecht entered the room, Father Val was unresponsive. Bishop Leibrecht touched him on the shoulder, then shook him several times, saying, "Father Val, can you hear me?" Finally, Father Val stirred and slowly opened his eyes. Bishop Leibrecht smiled and asked, "How are you doing?" Father Val responded, "Not so good. I was hoping to see Jesus, but it's you."

We want to see Jesus at the moment of death because God created us to be happy with him forever. But our forever has begun, and we want to be happy here and now.

Happiness, however, can be elusive. Famous entertainers search for happiness, only to be trapped in addictions that lead to premature, pitiful deaths. Talented athletes and well-known politicians seek happiness, but can end up betraying spouse and family in tawdry affairs that destroy careers and lives. If we want to avoid such mistakes, we must learn what happiness really is.

A good way to understand happiness is to realize that it exists at four levels and that knowing God's plan for our life can help us understand and enjoy them all. Happiness One, the satisfaction of physical appetites, involves only the body. A good meal, for example, brings pleasure and satisfaction. But a blind search for pleasure leads to addiction and frustration. So we move to the next level where mind and will direct the body to accomplish something worthwhile. This is Happiness Two, achievement and success. It is better than Happiness One, but it also has limits. Others surpass our achievements. Old age limits our abilities. Again, we look for more, and we find it in Happiness Three. Happiness Three involves the heart, raising us to a level where we find joy in loving others or serving a good cause. But even this level can fade, as friends move away and family members are taken from us by death. Is there more?

Yes. Happiness Four involves not only the body, mind, will, and heart, but the soul as well. We experience meaning, peace, and joy in knowing, loving, and serving God. Happiness Four does not lead to harmful addictions. Age doesn't cause it to fade, and it is not lessened by the achievements of others. God doesn't move away or die. Happiness Four surpasses all limits of the lower levels.

Even our own death does not put an end to Happiness Four. For those who follow Jesus, death is not an end, but a beginning. Death is birth to everlasting life. Saint Paul wrote: "But our citizenship is in heaven, and it is from there that we are expecting a Savior, the Lord Jesus Christ. He will transform the body of our humiliation that it may be conformed to the body of his glory, by the power that also enables him to make all things subject to himself" (Philippians 3:20–21).

DEATH AND LIFE AFTER DEATH

What happens at death? We leave our mortal, physical body for what may be called a spiritual body (see 1 Corinthians 15). The Bible teaches that we are judged after death in an experience traditionally named the particular judgment. If we die in union with God, with mind perfectly attuned to God's knowledge and with heart fully open to God's love, we enter heaven. If we are in union with God, but are not completely open to God's knowledge and love, we pass through a temporary period of purification, God's generous and loving gift of purgatory. Those who have rejected God by unrepented mortal sin have chosen hell, the awful state of eternal separation from God. At the end of time, there will be a general judgment, which will not change the outcome of the particular judgment, but will show how our lives fit into the totality of God's providential plan. The general judgment will also bring about the resurrection of the body, when we receive a new glorification that will remake our bodies after the pattern of Christ's glorified body. (For a more complete explanation of death and life after death, see Chapter 7 of my book, *We Believe...": A Survey of the Catholic Faith*).

HEAVEN

What is heaven? More glorious than our greatest imaginings, it is: "What no eye has seen, nor ear heard, nor the human heart conceived, what God has prepared for those who love him" (1 Corinthians 2:9). Heaven is being in the loving arms of God forever. It is freedom from sorrow, suffering, and death. It is perfect peace and security.

The greatest joy of heaven is what Father Val hoped for, to see Jesus. Jesus said: "Blessed are the pure in heart, for they will see God" (Matthew 5:8). Catholic tradition calls this sight the beatific vision because of the happiness it brings. What an incredible experience it will be to stand before God, to see Jesus, knowing that the love we've always wanted is ours forever.

To appreciate this, think about great moments of joy here on earth: parents holding their child for the first time, holidays with family, the company of friends, a safe landing, word from physicians that we are cured. If we put all these moments together, we can begin to imagine the happiness of heaven.

Prayer can offer a dramatic taste of heaven. Some saints have had moments of ecstasy at prayer that brought them near the gates of heaven. Saint Paul says he was "caught up to the third heaven—

whether in the body or out of the body I do not know....caught up into Paradise and heard things that cannot be told, that no mortal can repeat" (2 Corinthians 12:2–4).

PIE IN THE SKY?

Some atheists mock Christians for believing in heaven. They cynically call this belief, "pie in the sky." Is it foolish for us to spend our lives seeking to know, love, and serve God, hoping for eternal happiness in heaven? Are atheists right?

No. Jesus is right, and atheists are wrong in denying the existence of God and the reality of heaven. In Chapters 2 and 3 we discussed reasons for believing in God. These reasons are so compelling that they have led many intelligent scientists from atheism to belief. The God who touched their hearts is the same God who promises eternal life and has the power to bestow it upon us. Some of these former atheists were drawn to belief in God by experiences of life after death. Dr. Diane Komp turned from atheism to belief in the risen Jesus as the Savior who brings people through death to eternal life. Dr. Komp was touched by dying children, who had experienced heaven's glory in their passing from this life to the next. Dr. Howard Storm went through clinical death and found himself in hell. He came back a believer in God and eternal life!

There are many books, such as *Life After Life* by Dr. Raymond Moody, that relate the experiences of people who go through clinical death, leave the body, and enter a whole new world. I've met such individuals, and they have no doubt about the reality of heaven.

Scripture is clear in its proclamation of eternal life. Saint Paul was a persecutor of the first Christians. What turned him into a great preacher of the Gospel was a vision of the risen Jesus. Paul was absolutely certain of the reality of Christ's resurrection. He numbered more than five hundred eyewitnesses of the resurrection, and gave names of some of them. Paul was sure that we too will rise from the dead. He bluntly proclaimed: "If for this life only we have hoped in Christ, we are of all people most to be pitied. But in fact Christ has been raised from the dead, the first fruits of those who have died" (1 Corinthians 15:19–20).

The first Christians believed, as Catholics believe today, that heaven is real life. Those in heaven are aware of what happens on earth and can help us. Moses and Elijah appeared to Jesus on the Mount of Transfiguration (Matthew 17:1–9). After Christ's resurrection, saints whose tombs had been opened at the crucifixion appeared to believers, no doubt to give them courage and hope with the news of Christ's resurrection (Matthew 27:52–53).

We should not be surprised that heavenly life is all around us. Babies in the womb live a limited existence, unaware that a larger world surrounds and embraces them. When they die to life in the womb, they are born into our world. We live a limited physical existence in this world. When we die, we will be born into a much larger world of angels and saints and God, a world surrounding us even now with life and love.

CHRIST'S VICTORY

A mother in Broken Arrow, Oklahoma, told me that her six-year-old daughter, Karen, was sick and needed a shot. She assured Karen that it wouldn't hurt much and would make her feel better. Not long afterward, Karen's great-grandfather died. Karen was taken to the funeral home. She walked up to the casket and viewed the body. Then she asked her mother: "Is my great grandpa Ryan in heaven with my Father-God?" "Yes, he is," Mom replied. "Well," declared Karen, "my Father-God better give my great grandpa Ryan a shot, 'cause he don't look so good."

The sincerity and simplicity of Karen's faith should bring a smile to our face. It should also help us laugh at death, as Saint Paul did when he exulted in Christ's victory over death:

When this perishable body puts on imperishability, and this

mortal body puts on immortality, then the saying that is written will be fulfilled: "Death has been swallowed up in victory." "Where, O death, is your victory? Where, O death, is your sting?" ...But thanks be to God, who gives us the victory through our Lord Jesus Christ (1 Corinthians 15:54–55, 57).

TO BE HAPPY FOREVER

We began this book with a question, "Why did God make you?" We have considered the answer to that question and looked to the final goal for which God created us, "to be happy with him forever in heaven." We have studied many aspects of Catholic faith life: knowing God and the reasons to believe in God; being loved by God and loving God in return; living our faith by practicing virtue and rejecting sin; keeping the commandments; drawing close to God; finding assurance in the success of God's plan as it has been followed by those on earth and in heaven.

This plan of God is both beautiful and challenging. It may seem complex and a bit overwhelming. It's really not. It is meant to guide every human being, the wise and the simple, to eternal happiness. It can be summed up in two words, Jesus Christ.

Jesus is the Way, the Truth, and the Life. When we make it our life's business to know Jesus as he is found in history, in Scripture, and in the Church, we will achieve life's purpose. Jesus teaches us, as we've noted so often in this book, how to know, love, and serve God and to find happiness with God forever.

Trusting that Jesus will guide us through this life and lead us to heaven, we proclaim joyfully with Saint Paul:

I want to know Christ and the power of his resurrection and the sharing of his sufferings by becoming like him in his death, if somehow I may attain the resurrection from the dead. Not that I have already obtained this or have already reached the goal; but I press on to make it my own, because Christ Jesus has made me his own....forgetting what lies behind and straining forward to what lies ahead, I press on toward the goal for the prize of the heavenly call of God in Christ Jesus.

PHILIPPIANS 3:10–14

QUESTIONS FOR DISCUSSION AND REFLECTION

Can you give a brief summary of the four levels of happiness? What are your favorite sources of happiness at each level? Have you ever been with someone at the moment of death? Does death seem fearsome to you? How would you like to die? What aspect of heaven do you most anticipate? Do you agree that purgatory is "God's generous and loving gift"? Since every person is judged at the moment of death, what is the reason for the general judgment? Have you ever spoken with someone who doesn't believe in heaven or hell? How would you encourage them to believe in the reality of life after death? Do you pray often for a happy death?

ACTIVITIES

To read more about the reality and joys of heaven, see my books, *We Pray: Living in God's Presence* (Chapter 9) and *The Search For Happiness*, which explains the four levels of happiness in detail. Both books are published by Liguori.

Become aware of the presence of the risen Jesus. Speak to him in the words of John Cardinal Newman's prayer for a happy death:

> *Oh, my Lord and Savior,*
> *support me in that hour*
> *in the strong arms of Thy sacraments,*
> *and by the fresh fragrance of Thy consolations.*
> *Let the absolving words be said over me,*
> *and the holy oil sign and seal me,*

and Thy own Body be my food,
and Thy Blood my sprinkling;
and let my sweet Mother Mary breathe on me,
and my angel whisper peace to me,
and my glorious saints...smile upon me;
that in them all, and through them all,
I may receive the gift of perseverance,
and die, as I desire to live,
in Thy faith, in Thy Church,
in Thy service, and in Thy love. Amen.

WWW.NEWMANREADER.ORG/WORKS/
MEDITATIONS/MEDITATIONS8.HTML#DEATH

BIBLIOGRAPHY

Excerpts from the English translation of the *Catechism of the Catholic Church*, for the United States of America, 2nd ed., copyright © 1997, United States Catholic Conference, Inc.—Libreria Editrice Vaticana. Used with permission.

Frossard, Andre. *I Have Met Him: God Exists*. New York, New York: Herder and Herder, 1974.

International Committee on English in the Liturgy, National Conference of Catholic Bishops. *The Liturgy of the Hours*. New York: Catholic Book Publishing Company, 1975.

Jaki, Stanli L. *The Purpose of It All*. Washington, D.C., Regnery Gateway, 1990.

Komp, Diane M., MD. *Images of Grace*. Grand Rapids, MI: Zondervan Publishing House, 1996.

Lukefahr, Oscar. *A Catholic Guide to the Bible*. Revised Edition. Liguori, MO: Liguori Publications, 1998.

———. *Christ's Mother and Ours*. Revised Edition. Liguori, MO: Liguori Publications, 2003.

———. *The Privilege of Being Catholic*. Liguori, MO: Liguori Publications, 1993.

———. *The Search For Happiness*. Liguori, MO: Liguori Publications, 2002.

———. *"We Believe...": A Survey of the Catholic Faith*. Second Edition. Liguori, MO: Liguori Publications, 1995.

———. *We Pray: Living in God's Presence*. Liguori, MO: Liguori Publications, 2007.

———. *We Worship: A Guide to the Catholic Mass*. Liguori, MO: Liguori Publications, 2004.

Moody, Dr. Raymond A., Jr., MD. *Life After Life*. New York, NY, Bantam Books, 1975.

New Revised Standard Version of the Bible: Catholic Edition. Nashville, TN: Catholic Bible Press, 1993.

This We Believe, By This We Live. Revised Edition of the *Baltimore Catechism*. Confraternity of Christian Doctrine, 1954.

Wiesel, Elie. *Night*. Translated by Marion Wiesel. New York, NY: Hill and Wang, 2006.

INDEX